FamilyTime Bible Storybook

Presented To

_____

_____

From

_____

_____

On _____

Editorial staff

Founder, Dr. Henrietta Mears • **Publisher Emeritus,** William T. Greig • **Publisher, Children's Curriculum and Resources,** Lynnette Pennings, M.A. • **Senior Consulting Publisher,** Dr. Elmer L. Towns • **Managing Editor,** Sheryl Haystead • **Senior Consulting Editor,** Wesley Haystead, M.S.Ed. • **Senior Editor, Biblical and Theological Issues,** Bayard Taylor, M.Div. • **Editor,** Mary Gross Davis • **Contributing Editor,** Rachel Hong • **Designer,** Christina Renée Sharp

FamilyTime Bible Storybook

Gospel Light

Table of Contents

New Testament

To Parents

Welcome to the *FamilyTime Bible Storybook!* This book represents valuable investment potential that pays enormous dividends both in your child's life and your own life as well!

Studies have long shown that reading to our children is one of the most powerful ways we foster their own abilities as readers. Reading together is a warm, enjoyable family activity. Reading Bible stories is even more valuable, for the Word of God molds thinking and character, creating an eternal impact. The lively, interactive format of these Bible stories will involve every family member in reading, talking and praying together to help your family grow spiritually strong.

Here's how we suggest you use the *FamilyTime Bible Storybook:*

✝ Set aside a regular time to read a Bible story with your child. Consider making Bible story time part of your bedtime routine. Young children love the comfort and security that a bedtime routine provides. (They'll sleep better!)

✝ Find the interactive involvement instructions at the top of the page. Glance at the story to see where the action begins! As you begin the first interactive involvement, invite your child to imitate you. (They'll pick up on the fun right away!)

✝ Involve your older preschooler in answering the question(s) found at the bottom of the page. (Younger ones will gladly help *you* answer the question!)

✝ After reading the story (more than once if your child is interested), take a few minutes to relate the spiritual content of the Bible story to your child's own experiences. Ask several questions such as, **Who in this story showed love for God? Who obeyed God? What did (he) do? You can love and obey God, too. When can you obey God by (being kind)?**

✝ Pray with your child. Use simple words that he or she can understand. Thank God for His love and care and ask His help in everyday situations.

May God richly bless you and your family as you begin the great adventure of reading Bible stories together!

Old Testament

God Made the World

Genesis 1:1-19

Invite your child to do the illustrated motions with you.

God made the **world** to be big and round!
God made **sand** in the deserts and wet, squishy ground.

God made **hills** and valleys that go up and down.
God made **rocks** that are striped with red, black and brown.

God made **stars** that twinkle in the sky far away.
God made the bright **sun** that shines all day.

God made the **clouds** and the wide, wide sky.
God made big **mountains** that stand very high.

God made lots of water. He made oceans and streams.
God made wide **rivers** that are long and deep.

God made leafy **trees** that grow very tall.
He made flowers and **plants** that help feed us all.

God made the world for you and for me!
Thank You, God. There's so much to see!

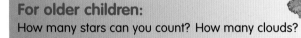

For older children:
How many stars can you count? How many clouds?

God Made Animals

Genesis 1:20-25

As you read the story, invite your child to join you in making the suggested motions and sounds.

God made a big world. It had mountains and trees. It had oceans and lakes. It was beautiful! But no fish swam in the water. No birds flew in the sky. **Shake head no**.

So God said, "Let there be fish and all kinds of living things in the water!" And little shiny fish wiggled in the water. Big red fish and blue fish and yellow fish wiggled in the water. **Wiggle hands**.

Sea horses bobbed up and down. **Bob hands**.

Big whales and dolphins jumped out of the water. **Jump hands**.

God also said, "Let there be birds of all kinds!"

And big eagles spread their wings wide. **Spread arms**.

Little birds of every color chirped and pecked at the ground. **Chirp**.

Chickens clucked as they walked. **Cluck**.

Ducks floated on the water and quacked. **Quack**.

Now the water was filled with moving fish and sea animals!

The trees and sky were full of singing birds. But God wasn't finished!

God said, "Let there be animals on the land!"

And horses ran and neighed in the grasslands. **Neigh**.

Cows mooed and chewed. **Moo**. Cats meowed. **Meow**.

They chased squeaky mice. **Squeak**. Bears growled. **Growl**.

Lions and tigers roared. **Roar**.

The world was full of moving noisy animals!

God had filled the ocean with fish and other creatures.

He had filled the trees and sky with all sorts of birds.

He had filled the land with animals.

God looked at what He had made. It was good!

For older children: Name in ABC order as many animals as you can!

God Made People

Genesis 1:26-31; 2:7-23; 3:20

Invite your child to count on fingers
(or make a zero with fingers)
with you as you read the story.

One God made the whole world!

He made the sky, the clouds and the water, all **three**!

God made mountains and deserts, valleys and hills.

Those are **four** kinds of places.

God made trees and bushes and grasses—**three** kinds of plants.

Next He made **two** big lights—the sun and moon.

Then God made fish, birds and other animals, **three** more kinds of living things.

But in this **one** wonderful world full of lively things, there was **no one** for God to talk with.

There was **no one** to take care of what He had made.

So God did **one** more thing. God made a man. He named the man Adam.

God gave Adam a job. Adam started naming all of the animals God had made!

But God knew Adam needed **one** more person to love and talk to. So God made a woman.

He brought her to Adam. Adam named her Eve.

Now there were **two** people. God told them, "Have children!

And take care of the animals and birds and everything you see in My world.

So Adam and Eve worked together. They were happy to do what God told them.

God was glad He had made **one** world, **two** people and many living things!

For older children: How high can you count on your fingers? How high can you count if you count on your toes, too?

12

God Loves Adam and Eve

Imitate the face by each paragraph as you read.
Invite your child to join you.

Genesis 2:16-17; 3

God's world was beautiful. It was filled with animals and birds, trees and flowers.
There was good fruit to eat everywhere! God put Adam and Eve in a beautiful garden.
Adam and Eve were happy! They loved to take care of the garden.
They loved God and God loved them.

happy

The garden had many trees in it. But God showed Adam one special tree.
God said, "You may eat from all the other trees here.
But DO NOT eat from this special tree."

serious

Then one day, a beautiful snake came to the garden. The snake was really God's enemy, Satan.
Satan told Eve, "You can eat the fruit from the special tree." Eve listened to Satan.
She looked at the fruit on that tree. She picked it. She bit into it.
She gave some to Adam. Adam ate it, too.

sneaky

As soon as Adam and Eve ate that fruit, they knew they
had done wrong.
They felt sad. They ran away and hid. God called, "Adam, where are you?"
Adam said, "I was hiding. I was afraid."

sad

God was very sad that Adam and Eve had disobeyed.
God told them they must leave the beautiful garden.
But God never stopped loving them. God gave them a happy promise.
Many years later, God kept that promise. God sent His Son, Jesus, to forgive
people for the wrong things we do when we don't obey God's rules.

hopeful

For older children: How many pieces of red fruit can you count?
How many pieces of yellow fruit? How many blueberries?

13

Building the Big Boat

Genesis 6:5-22

As you read the story, invite your child to guess the second word in each rhyming pair.

God had made a happy world. It was very **good**.
But people had stopped doing all the good things that they **should**.

Instead, they hurt each other. People did things that were **mean**.
God grew very sad about the mean things He had **seen**.

God decided it was time. He'd have to send a **flood**.
There would be a lot of rain. There'd be a lot of **mud**.

God told a man named Noah, "This is what I'm going to **do**.
I'm going to send a flood. But Noah, here's a job for **you**!

I want you to build a boat, so tall, this wide, that **deep**.
The boat will hold the animals that I want you to **keep**.

The boat will hold your family and everything you'll **need**
To keep the animals and yourselves safe and well **indeed**!"

Noah listened to the Lord—remembered every **word**.
Noah started working to do everything he'd **heard**.

His family cut a lot of trees. They sawed a lot of **wood**.
They pounded boards and put on tar and did just what they **should**.

God helped them know just what to do. They worked very **hard**.
They were glad to do good things and obey the **Lord**!

For older children: Find items in the picture that begin with the "B" sound.

14

Loading the Big Boat

Genesis 7:1-16

Point to the pictures and let your child help you tell the story.

[Picture key: Noah, Noah's wife, Noah's family, big boat, water, animals, food, bears, birds, rabbits, elephants]

Here is [Noah]. Here is [Noah's wife]. Here is [Noah's family]. Here is the [big boat] God told [Noah] to build.

Why did they need such a [big boat]? God had a big plan for the [big boat].

God was going to send a flood of [water]. But God planned for the [big boat] to hold two of every kind of animal! God's plan would save [Noah] and [Noah's wife] and [Noah's family] and all the [animals] from the [water] when it started to rain.

[Noah] and [Noah's wife] and [Noah's family] worked together. They built a big ramp. Then they brought baskets and baskets of [food] up the ramp into the [big boat].

Then God told [Noah], "In a week, it will start to rain. [water] will start to rise. Bring all the [animals] into the [big boat]." [Noah's family] worked very hard! There were [bears] that needed to find a place to sleep. [birds] needed places to nest. [rabbits] hopped up the ramp. [elephants] walked slowly up the ramp and into the [big boat]. There were MANY [animals] to bring! But finally every one of the [animals] was safe in the [big boat].

[Noah] and [Noah's wife] and [Noah's family] got into the [big boat], too. Then God closed the door. Everyone could rest now! God had helped [Noah's family] do good things, even though it was hard work!

For older children: Act like one of the [animals] that came into the [big boat]. See who in your family can guess what animal you are acting like!

15

Safe in the Boat

Genesis 7:17—8:14

Invite your child to tell the story by describing what is happening in each picture. Say, "This is a story that has no words. We'll tell the story together!" Check the Bible passage if you need more information.

For older children: Tell the story again by yourself. Ask your parent to record your story, so you can play it later!

God Sends a Rainbow

Genesis 8:15-22; 9:8-17

As you read, make the motions indicated.
Invite your child to imitate you.

For days and days and days, it had rained and rained and rained.

Make falling rain with fingers.

Noah and his family and all the animals were still safe in the big boat.

But now the rain had stopped. Noah and his family must have been GLAD! **Clap.**

The people and animals in the big boat were probably TIRED of rain!

Every day, the water from the flood went down and down and down.

Move hand down.

One day, Noah felt a BUMP! The big boat was on dry ground!

Now there were places for the animals to live. **Point outside.**

So Noah, his wife and his family began to let the animals out.

The big door opened. The animals began to walk down the ramp. **Walk fingers.**

Here came big bears moving slowly. Little squirrels jumped and ran.

Monkeys and mice, lions and lizards ran and bounced. **Jump fingers.**

Ducks and dogs waddled and trotted. Birds flew away, higher and higher.

Then Noah and his family walked out. The sunshine felt warm and good! **Look up.**

Noah said, "God took care of us all this long rainy time! Let's thank Him!"

Noah's family prayed and thanked God. **Fold hands in prayer.**

God made a promise to Noah and his family.

God promised, "I will never cover the world with water again. **Point to sky.**

I will put something in the sky to help you remember My promise."

Noah's family looked at the sky. **Look up.**

They could see beautiful colors! It was a rainbow!

God helped Noah and his family and all the animals.

Noah and his family were glad to thank God!

For older children: See how many things you can name that are the same colors as the colors in a rainbow.

17

Abraham Obeys God

Genesis 12:1-8

Walk your fingers every time you read about walking. Invite your child to imitate you.

Abraham lived in a city. He lived in a house.
One day, God told Abraham, "I want you to move to a new land.
I will show you how to get there." There were no cars,
airplanes or trains. Abraham would have to walk.

Abraham chose to obey God.
He told his wife, Sarah, and his nephew Lot,
    "We are going to leave this city. We are going to a new land."
Abraham and his family would need strong sandals for walking!

The family had sheep, goats and cows. They had
    camels and donkeys.
They worked hard to get the animals ready.
They packed food and clothes and sandals.
They packed up tents and blankets for sleeping.

Then they started walking.
What kinds of noises do you think their walking sandals made?
Step, step, step. Walk, walk, walk. They walked every day.
Every night they got out their tents and blankets.
They took off their sandals and rubbed their tired feet.
The new land was far, far away from the city.
But they knew God was taking care of them. So they kept walking.

One day, God told Abraham, "This place will be your new home."
Abraham and his family put up their tents.
They thanked God for keeping them safe all the way to this new land.
God was glad Abraham had obeyed. Abraham was glad, too.
Now he and his family were done walking! They could rest their feet!

For older children: What different kinds of shoes do you have? Why do you think there are different kinds of shoes?

Lot Chooses First

Genesis 13

Read words in red in a loud voice. Read words in blue in a quiet voice. Invite your child to join you.

Abraham and his nephew Lot lived near each other. They both had many sheep that said "BAAAH!" They both had cows that said "MOO!" very loudly. Both had donkeys that went "HEE-HAAW!" all the time. Both had goats that said "NAAAAH! NAAAAH!" day and night. And they had camels that GRUNTED and SNUFFLED. There were many noisy animals!

But the animals weren't the ONLY ones making noise. There was not enough food and water for all the animals. So the helpers who took care of Abraham's animals and the helpers who took care of Lot's animals were making noise, too!

Abraham's helpers talked loudly to Lot's helpers: "Move AWAY! There is not enough water for all your animals, too!"

Lot's helpers talked even MORE loudly: "WE were here first! WE need this grass. YOU move on!" Soon there were many loud angry voices!

Abraham said, "We must not fight. We need to move away from each other, so there will be enough grass and water for all these animals! "So Abraham and Lot climbed a hill to look at all the land around them.

Abraham told Lot, "You may choose first, Lot. Choose the land you want."

Lot pointed toward the flat land that had lots of grass. "I'll move down there," Lot said.

Lot took his family, his helpers AND his animals—sheep that said "BAAAH!"—cows that said "MOO!"—donkeys that went "HEE-HAAW!"—goats that said "NAAAAH! NAAAAH!" and camels that GRUNTED and SNUFFLED—to the land with lots of green grass.

Abraham and his family, his helpers and his animals went to live in the land that didn't have as much grass. But Abraham knew God would take care of him AND all of his sheep that said "BAAAH!"—cows that said "MOO"—donkeys that went "HEE HAAW!"—goats that said "NAAAAH! NAAAAH!"—and camels that GRUNTED and SNUFFLED.

For older children: Think of three animals not in this picture. What sounds do they make? Are those sounds like the sounds of any animals that are in the picture?

Isaac Is Born

Genesis 17:15-19; 18:1-15; 21:1-8

As you read, invite your child
to do the actions with you.

Abraham and Sarah were very, very old. **Hold up two fingers**.

But God had promised them a baby to hold! **Rock a baby**.

Abraham laughed when he heard this news. **Laugh**.

But God had made a promise. God's promises are true!

Sign "true."

Three visitors came to see Abraham one day.

Hold up three fingers.

Abraham and Sarah invited them to stay. **Motion "come here."**

One visitor was God, who had promised them a son.

Hold up one finger.

He told Abraham again that a son would be born. **Nod**.

Now Sarah laughed, too. How could such a thing be? **Laugh**.

But God said, "NOTHING is too hard for Me! **Shake head no**.

Next year you and Sarah WILL have a son!" **Nod**.

And just as God promised, baby Isaac was born! **Rock a baby**.

Baby Isaac giggled. Baby Isaac smiled. **Smile**.

He yawned and he wiggled and even when he cried,

Pretend to yawn.

Abraham and Sarah were glad to have their son. **Hug self**.

God kept His promise! See what God had done! **Nod**. **Rock baby**.

For older children: God promised Abraham that he would have as many children and grandchildren as there are stars in the sky. How many stars can you count in the picture?

Eliezer Prays

Genesis 24

As you read, make the motions for each colored word. Invite your child to imitate you.

Look

Smile

Walk

Pray

Isaac was all grown up! His father, Abraham, was very, very old.
He wanted to **look** for a wife for Isaac. Abraham had a helper named Eliezer.
He told his helper, "Go to the town where my relatives live.
Look for a wife for Isaac. God will help you."

Eliezer packed his things on camels. He got on a camel.
The camels **walked** and **walked**. While the camels **walked**, Eliezer must have
said to himself, *How can I look for the right woman to be Isaac's wife?*
He **smiled**. He had an idea. He could **pray**!

So Eliezer **prayed**, "God, please help me find a wife for Isaac. Let the woman
You have chosen give me a drink. And let her gladly give my camels a drink, too."

Eliezer was near the town Abraham told him about.
He got off his camel near the well.
He **looked** and saw a beautiful young woman. She filled her pitcher with water.
Eliezer asked her for a drink. She gave him a drink.
Then she said, "I'll give water to your camels, too."

Eliezer must have **smiled** and **smiled**!
The girl's name was Rebekah. She brought him to her house.
He asked if Rebekah would go with him to marry Isaac. Rebekah said yes!

Soon, Eliezer and Rebekah got on the camels that **walked** and **walked** back
to where Isaac lived! Isaac and Rebekah got married and EVERYONE **smiled**!

For older children: Which camel is biggest? Which camel has the most bells on its harness?

Jacob and Esau

Count on your fingers when you read the words **one** or **two**. Wiggle your fingers when you read the word **many**. Invite your child to join you.

Genesis 25:19-28

Isaac was **one** man who loved God. Isaac married **one** lady named Rebekah. For a long time, these two had no children. That must have made Isaac and Rebekah sad. Isaac prayed and asked God to give them children.

God answered Isaac's prayer. Soon, Rebekah was going to have **one** baby! Then God told Rebekah something surprising: She was going to have twins. Isaac and Rebekah were going to have TWO babies!

Many days passed. **One** day it was time for the twins to be born—**one**, two. The twins were both boys. Some twins look alike, and some twins even act alike. But these twins were very different from each other. **One** boy was very red when he was born. He had lots of hair. Isaac and Rebekah named him Esau.

The other baby was born right after Esau. This **one** wasn't red like Esau. He had smooth skin. He didn't have a lot of hair. His parents named him Jacob. These two boys were very different from each other.

As the two boys grew, Esau and Jacob still were different in **many** ways. They didn't look like each other. They didn't act like each other. Esau was strong. He liked to be outdoors. He loved to hunt with his bow and **many** arrows. Isaac must have been very proud of his big, strong son, Esau.

Jacob liked to stay home in the tents where his family lived. He liked to cook **many** foods. His mother, Rebekah, must have been very proud of her **one** quiet, helpful son, Jacob.

Isaac and Rebekah were very happy that God gave them two sons to love.

For older children: Name as many family members as you can. Ask a grown-up to help you.

An Unfair Trade

Genesis 25:27-34

We're **twins**. But we're not alike **at all!**

I'm Esau. I'm older.
I love to hunt and be **outdoors**.

I'm Jacob. I like to stay home.
And I'm a **good cook!**

I have the birthright because I'm **older**.

That means that someday he'll be the leader of our family.
He'll get most of what our father, Isaac, owns.

Jacob will get less.
And he WON'T be the leader because he's **younger**.

Years later these brothers made a trade. Here's how it happened:

I've been hunting for a long time.
I'm **VERY hungry!**

Sniff! Sniff! Wow!
That smells GOOD!
Give me some stew!

I'm not going to share.
He has to pay!

First, give me your birthright.
THEN I'll give you **stew to eat**.

I'm going to DIE if I don't eat.
That birthright won't help me then!
You can HAVE my birthright.
Now give me **some STEW!**

Ha! Now I'll get the MOST!
I'll get to be **the leader!**

Yum!

The trade was done.
Now Jacob had the birthright.
And Esau had stew!
Jacob was unkind, but we can be kind.

For older children: Name all the foods you find in the pictures.

Isaac Digs Wells

Genesis 26:12-33

Wiggle your fingers whenever you read the word water. Invite your child to join you.

Isaac grew lots of food and many animals, too.

Isaac and his family and all his animals needed water.

Isaac's helpers dug wells. They found water!

But the neighbors who lived nearby got angry.

They didn't want Isaac to have that water.

They said the water was theirs!

Isaac did not argue about the water.

He showed love. He moved away.

Isaac's helpers dug more wells in the new place.

They found water again!

But the angry neighbors wanted THAT water, too.

So Isaac moved again. His helpers dug another well.

More water! And no one came to argue about
   THIS water! WHEW!

But one day, the neighbors came to see Isaac.

Did they want to argue? No!

They told Isaac, "We know that God is with you.

We will not take your water anymore.

We don't want to argue with you.

We want to be friends."

Isaac made a big dinner for the neighbors.

Everyone was happy!

For older children: How many times can you find the word water on this page? Look in the picture, too!

Jacob's Tricks

Genesis 27:1-45

Pause before you read the second word in each rhyming pair. Let your child guess the rhyming word.

Isaac was the father. Rebekah was the mother.
They had twin sons. Each one was a **brother**.
One son was Jacob. He took more than his share.
He had taken Esau's birthright. He really wasn't fair.
But now, father Isaac had grown old and couldn't see.
He said, "I must bless Esau, while it still can **be**."

Well, Jacob and Rebekah overheard Isaac's plan.
The two of them decided to fool this old **man**.
Jacob had the birthright. He'd get the blessing, too.
He didn't care if the things he said were true.
Jacob and his mother got skins from a goat.
They made him feel hairy. Then he put on Esau's **coat**.

Now Jacob smelled like Esau. He felt like Esau, too.
To his poor blind father, Jacob took a bowl of **stew**.
Isaac was thinking something might be wrong.
He said, "Are you really Esau, Esau big and strong?
You feel and smell like Esau. I can touch you, standing near.
But you don't sound like Esau. It is Jacob's voice I **hear**!"

But Jacob was sure he could fool his old dad.
He didn't tell the truth. The thing he did was **bad**.
Father Isaac was fooled. He blessed his younger son.
When Esau came back home, he found he'd blessed the wrong one!
Esau was so angry! Esau was so sad!
He cried because his blessing went to Jacob. He was **mad**!

Now Jacob was afraid. He would have to run away.
Many years would pass before he could come home to **stay**.
Everyone was hurt when Jacob told what was not true.
But we can tell the truth. It makes us happy, me and you!

For older children: With a grown-up, say all the pairs of rhyming words in the poem. Can you think of more rhyming words?

Esau Forgives Jacob

Genesis 32:3-21; 33:1-11

Hold two fingers together when you read the word **brothers**. Walk your fingers when you read words about **walking**. Run your fingers when you read words about running. Invite your child to imitate you.

Jacob and Esau were **brothers.** But Jacob had tricked their father. Jacob got important things Esau should have been given. Esau was angry! And Jacob was afraid. So Jacob **ran** far away. He stayed away for many YEARS. He got married and had many children.

But one day, God told Jacob it was time to go home. Jacob and his family and animals and helpers **walked** the long way back. Was Jacob's **brother** Esau still angry? Jacob sent helpers to find out. They **ran** back to tell him, "Esau is **walking** this way. He has 400 men with him!"

Was Esau going to HURT them? Jacob PRAYED! He asked God to keep him and his family safe.

Then he decided, *I'll send my **brother** some GIFTS! That should help him not to be angry.*

Jacob chose goats and sheep and camels. He sent groups of them **walking** along the road. Then he sent herds of cattle and donkeys **walking** ahead! Jacob and his family **walked** FAR behind the animals.

Finally, they could SEE Esau and his men! Jacob **walked** toward Esau, far ahead of his family. He bowed low, over and over. Jacob looked up. Esau was RUNNING toward Jacob. Oh! Was Esau going to HURT him?

No! What did Esau do? Esau HUGGED Jacob! He KISSED him! The two **brothers** cried and hugged. They forgave each other! Jacob wasn't afraid any more. The **brothers** were glad to see each other again!

For older children: How many sheep can you count? How many cows? How many animals are there all together?

Joseph and His Brothers

Genesis 37

Invite your child to imitate the faces next to the paragraphs as you read.

My name is Joseph. I have 10 big brothers and 1 little brother.
My father, Jacob, loves me! He gave me a colorful coat.

I had dreams about my family.
The dreams said my family would bow to me.
Do you think the dreams mean I will be in charge someday?

We are Joseph's big brothers.
We have no colorful coats!
We don't want to bow to Joseph!
Joseph and his dreams make us ANGRY!

One day we took our family's sheep out to find grass.
We were gone a long time.
Guess who our father sent to see if we were working hard.
JOSEPH! We were NOT glad to see him!

I walked and walked to find my brothers.
They must have seen me from a long way off.
My coat made them ANGRY. My dreams made them ANGRY.
So when I walked up, they grabbed me.
They threw me in a PIT! I was sad.

Ha! Joseph was in the pit. And we saw traders coming on their camels.
(Traders are people who buy and sell things.)
We pulled Joseph out of the pit and SOLD him!
Now Joseph was gone! We were GLAD!
We tore his colorful coat. We put animal's blood on it.
HA! Our father would think a wild animal had KILLED Joseph!

I was taken far away to Egypt by the traders. I was sold to be a slave.
(A slave is a person who is owned by someone else.) I was AFRAID.
But even when I was in Egypt, I knew God was with me.

For older children: How many brothers or sisters do you have? How many cousins? Grandparents?

Joseph in Prison

Genesis 39—40

Invite your child to say the repeating phrases with you.

Joseph was sold to be a slave. But he kept on **doing what is right**.
Joseph worked hard for Potiphar, **every day and every night**.

Potiphar's wife lied about Joseph. But he kept on **doing what is right**.
Joseph went to jail and stayed there, **every day and every night**.

Joseph worked hard in jail. He kept on **doing what is right**.
Joseph was soon put in charge, **every day and every night**.

Joseph helped Pharaoh's sad cupbearer. Joseph kept on **doing what is right**.
The cupbearer dreamed a strange dream one night. He wondered what it meant.

God helped Joseph understand the dream. And Joseph kept on **doing what is right**.
The cupbearer would go back to work, after three days and three nights.

The words that Joseph said were true! And he kept on **doing what is right**.
The cupbearer left. He was happy! But he forgot Joseph, **every day and every night**.

So Joseph stayed there in the jail. But he kept on **doing what is right**.
He knew God would be with him, **every day and every night**.

For older children: Name three things you do every day and every night.

Joseph Forgives His Family

Invite your child to trace the path to follow the story action.

Genesis 42:1-8; 43:16; 45; 46:5-7

Joseph's family lived in Canaan. No rain had fallen for a long time.
Food stopped growing! Joseph's family was hungry!

Jacob, Joseph's father, heard that in Egypt there was grain.
So he told his sons to go to Egypt. The brothers packed.
The brothers walked. Egypt was a LONG way off!

After days and DAYS, they came to Egypt.
They found the leader who sold grain.
This man looked Egyptian. This man spoke Egyptian.
But this man was their brother JOSEPH!

Joseph knew his brothers right away.
But he didn't tell them who he was—not yet.
He sold them sacks and sacks of grain.

Then the brothers packed. The brothers walked.
Canaan was a LONG way off!

They finally got home with the grain to use to make food.
After it was eaten, they needed more!
So the brothers packed to go back to Egypt.
The brothers walked. Egypt was a LONG way off!

After days and DAYS, they were back in Egypt.
Then Joseph surprised them! He said, "I'm your brother Joseph!" The brothers didn't smile.
They were afraid! They had done bad things to Joseph! Would Joseph now be mean?

NO! Joseph hugged each brother. He forgave them.
He gave them grain and told them, "Come back to Egypt to live!"
The brothers packed. The brothers walked. Canaan was a LONG way off!
Then the family packed. The whole family walked. Egypt was STILL a LONG way off!

But finally, Jacob and all of Joseph's family were in Egypt.
Everyone was glad Joseph showed love!

For older children: Imagine you are walking on a long trip. What would you take with you? What would you wear?

30

Baby in a Basket

Exodus 1:8—2:10

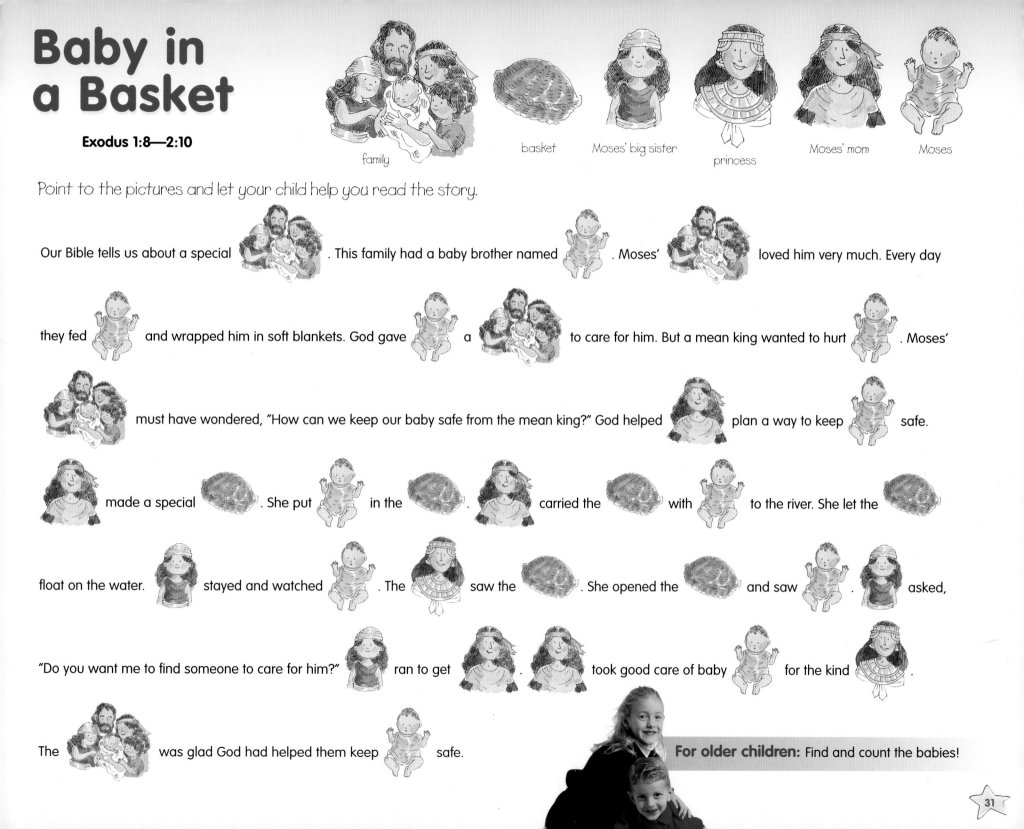

family · basket · Moses' big sister · princess · Moses' mom · Moses

Point to the pictures and let your child help you read the story.

Our Bible tells us about a special [family]. This family had a baby brother named [Moses]. Moses' [family] loved him very much. Every day

they fed [Moses] and wrapped him in soft blankets. God gave [family] a [family] to care for him. But a mean king wanted to hurt [Moses]. Moses'

[family] must have wondered, "How can we keep our baby safe from the mean king?" God helped [Moses' mom] plan a way to keep [Moses] safe.

[Moses' mom] made a special [basket]. She put [Moses] in the [basket]. [Moses' mom] carried the [basket] with [Moses] to the river. She let the [basket]

float on the water. [Moses' big sister] stayed and watched [Moses]. The [princess] saw the [basket]. She opened the [basket] and saw [Moses]. [Moses' big sister] asked,

"Do you want me to find someone to care for him?" [Moses' big sister] ran to get [Moses' mom]. [Moses' mom] took good care of baby [Moses] for the kind [princess].

The [family] was glad God had helped them keep [Moses] safe.

For older children: Find and count the babies!

31

Escape from Egypt

Invite your child to repeat the words VERY long trip with you.

Exodus 12:31-38; 13:20-22

God's people went on a VERY long trip.
God was leading His people to a brand-new home.
Moses knew God would be with them
All the way on this VERY long trip.

"We'll need food to eat," the people said.
They packed up food for this VERY long trip.
"We'll need water," the people said.
They filled water bags for this VERY long trip.

"We'll need tents and blankets, so we can sleep.
We'll need to rest on this VERY long trip!"
They packed up tents and blankets.
They gathered sheep and goats.
Now they were ready—
    ready to go on their VERY long trip.

God's people started out
    on the VERY long trip.
Moses told them,
    "God will lead us.

He will be with us on our VERY long trip.
    God will take care of us and show us
        where to go."

God put a big white cloud in the sky.
The people followed the cloud.
The cloud led the people every day—
Every day of the VERY long trip.

At night, God put a fire in the sky.
The fire showed the people that God
    was with them.
Every night, God's fire gave them light—
Every night on the VERY long trip.

Everywhere the people went
They saw the cloud. They saw the fire.
The people knew that God was with them
All the time on the VERY long trip!

For older children: Count the animals
in the picture.

32

A Path Through the Sea

Exodus 14:1—15:20

As you read the words step-by-step, you and your child move your fingers as though they are walking.

Where could all God's people go,
step-by-step, step-by-step?
Moses said, "Let's cross the sea.
God told me what to do."

What did they hear, step-by-step so fast?
Horses' hooves! Marching feet!
The mean king and his army came,
step-by-step, step-by-step!

God's people traveled,
step-by-step, step-by-step, step-by-step.
Following the cloud God sent,
they camped beside the sea.

Moses walked up to the sea step-by-step, step-by-step.
He raised his hand and strong winds blew,
wildly roaring through!

Bit by bit, the sea got dry;
water piled very high!

Step-by-step, the people
walked right through the sea!

When Moses raised his hand again,
the water came together—CRASH!

God's people were all safe again,
walking step-by-step!

The people stopped their walk to sing,
thank the Lord and dance for joy.

Then laughing, singing, they walked on,
step-by-step, step-by-step!

For older children: How many feet can you count?

33

Crossing the Jordan

Joshua 3—4:18

Make the following motions as you read. Invite your child to imitate you.

 amazing   river   no   stopped   walk, walked

God's people had **walked** a long, long way. They were near the land God had promised to give them. God had done an **amazing** thing to help them escape from their own land.

Now God's people were camped by the Jordan **River**. The land God had promised to give them was across this **river**. But the water in the **river** was high. It was fast. It was scary! How would the people get across? They had **no** boats. There were **no** bridges. **No** one could SWIM across that fast **river!**

Joshua told the people, "Get ready to cross the **river**. Tomorrow you will see God do more **amazing** things!" People rolled up their tents and packed their things. What **amazing** things would God do?

Joshua told the people, "**Walk** behind the Ark of the Lord!" (The Ark of the Lord was a beautiful golden box that reminded the people that God was with them.) Men carried the Ark to the edge of the rushing **river**. When their toes touched the **river**, God **stopped** the water! Many miles upstream, the water stood up like a big wall! God had done another **AMAZING** thing!

The men stood with the Ark in the middle of the riverbed. The people **walked** around them to the other side. Each family leader **stopped** to pull a big stone from the riverbed.

Everyone was safely across the **river**. God told Joshua, "Tell the men carrying the Ark to walk up out of the Jordan." The men **walked** out of the riverbed. WHOOSH! The water ROARED back! The **river** was full of rushing water again!

Joshua and the people stacked up the stones from the riverbed. Whenever they saw those stones, they would tell the story of how God brought them to the land He promised to give them. God did an **AMAZING** thing!

For older children: What is something there is only one of in the picture? Two? Three? Four? Five?

35

Walls Fall Down

Invite your child to join you in this finger play.

Joshua 6

We're marching around Jericho,
We're marching around Jericho,
We're marching around Jericho—
We'll march for six days. 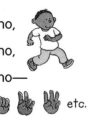 etc.

The priests are marching with their horns,
The priests are marching with their horns,
The priests are marching with their horns—
We hear the toot, toot, toot.

But on the SEVENTH day . . .
We're marching around Jericho,
We're marching around Jericho—
We're marching SEVEN times! etc.

The priests are marching with their horns,
The priests are marching with their horns,
The priests are marching with their horns—
When they BLOW them, then we SHOUT! Yea!

The walls are falling down right now,
The walls are falling down right now,
The walls are falling down right now—
Just as God said they would!

For older children: How many times can you find "W" in the poem?
In the picture?

Deborah Obeys God

Judges 4:1-16; 5:4,20-21

God's people were **not** obeying God.

They had **big** trouble!

An army with 900 chariots wanted to **fight** them.

The people of Israel finally **prayed** to God.

God gave Deborah a **message** for Barak (BAHR-ehk):

"God says: 'Get 10,000 men.

I will **help** you defeat that **big** army.'"

Barak was **afraid** to obey God!

So he said, "Deborah, **if** you go with me, I will **go**.

But **if** you don't go, I **won't** go."

Deborah wanted Barak to **trust** God and obey.

So she told him, "I **will** go with you."

Barak asked God's **people** to help.

Soon **10,000** men came.

Deborah and Barak led the soldiers up Mount Tabor.

They **looked** out across the flat land.

Nine hundred **chariots** were coming closer and **closer**.

Deborah told Barak, "**Go**! God will help you. You will **win**!"

Just THEN, **God** sent a thunderstorm!

Lightning flashed. **Rain** poured.

The chariots all got **stuck** in the MUD!

God helped Deborah and Barak,

just as He said He would do!

Deborah and Barak **sang** about how God won the battle!

Their song is written down in the Bible.

Everyone **praised** God!

Deborah and Barak were **glad** they had obeyed God.

For older children: Make the sounds you hear during a big storm. How many different sounds can you make?

37

Ruth Loves Naomi

Ruth 1—2

Follow the grains of barley to read the story.
Invite your child to trace the path with you.

My name is Ruth.
Naomi is my mother-in-law.

We had no food. We had no way to grow food or to get money to buy food.

Now I am picking up as much barley as I can to share with Naomi. We'll make food from the barley.

It takes a long time to pick up every little grain. It is hard work. But I am glad to help Naomi. She has been kind to me. I want to be kind to her.

Ruth is very kind. She is patient. I am glad she is sharing with Naomi.

Here is barley, Naomi! Now we can make good food to eat!

Please take barley from my field whenever you need it. Drink water from my water jars.

For older children: How many things in the picture begin with the "B" sound?

Hannah's Prayer

1 Samuel 1; 2:18-19

Encourage your child to make a face
or a motion to show the words.

A lady named Hannah lived long ago, and she wasn't very glad.
Hannah had no children, and that made her sad!
Make a sad face.

Hannah stood in the Tabernacle and quietly cried.
She wanted a baby! She prayed and she sighed.
Pretend to pray.

Hannah prayed to the Lord, "Please give me a son.
I'll teach him to love You, if You'll give me one."
Hold up one finger.

A teacher named Eli talked to Hannah that day.
He said, "God will give what you've asked is what I'll pray."
Point upward.

Hannah knew God had listened. She knew God is good.
Soon God's answer came, like she knew it would.
Pretend to rock baby.

Baby Samuel was born; Hannah stopped being sad.
Now she had a son; she was excited and glad.
Make a happy face.

Samuel soon learned how to run, jump and play.
Then Hannah took him to old Eli, where Samuel would stay.
Wave good-bye.

Every year Hannah brought a new coat for her son.
She prayed and thanked God for all He had done.
Say "Thank you!"

For older children: How many smiling faces can you count? Sad faces?

Helping at the Tabernacle

1 Samuel 1:28; 2:11,18-21,26

Invite your child to act out the actions described in the story.

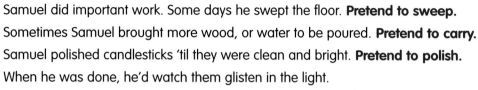

When Samuel was a little boy, he woke up, just like you,
Early in the morning, when the day was brand new. **Stretch arms.**
Samuel pulled his clothes on; he put on his sandal shoes. **Pretend to dress.**
He hurried to eat breakfast, and here's what he would do. **Pretend to eat.**

Samuel did important work. Some days he swept the floor. **Pretend to sweep.**
Sometimes Samuel brought more wood, or water to be poured. **Pretend to carry.**
Samuel polished candlesticks 'til they were clean and bright. **Pretend to polish.**
When he was done, he'd watch them glisten in the light.

When everything was ready and Eli told him "Now's the time,"
Samuel pushed the great big doors until they opened wide.
Pretend to push doors.
Then people came to worship God; they came inside to pray.
Pretend to pray.
And Samuel knew he'd done good work each and every day.

Every year, his mother came to visit Samuel and brought him new clothes. **Pretend to put on coat.**
As Samuel got bigger, she loved to watch him grow! **Move hand to show increasing height.**
Samuel worked and grew and learned, and everyone was glad
To see him do his very best and learn to obey God!

For older children: How many triangles can you find in the pictures? How many circles?

Samuel Listens and Obeys

1 Samuel 3

When you say the word **called**, help your child cup hands around mouth.
When you say the words **hear** or **listen**, encourage your child to cup a hand by ear.

One night when Samuel was asleep, he **heard** a voice **call** his name. "Samuel!"
Samuel got right up and ran to Eli. "Here I am, Eli! Did you **call** me?"
Eli said, "I didn't **call** you, Samuel. Go back to bed."
Samuel obeyed. He crawled back into bed.

Then he **heard** that voice again. "Samuel!"
Samuel jumped out of bed and ran to Eli.
"Here I am, Eli! Did you **call** me?" Samuel said.
Eli said, "I didn't **call** you, Samuel. Go back to bed."

Soon the voice came again.
Samuel got right up and ran to Eli.
"Here I am, Eli! Did you **call** me?" Samuel said.
This time Eli told Samuel, "If you **hear** the voice again, say this: 'Speak, Lord. I'm **listening**.' "
Samuel obeyed. He crawled back into bed.

Soon he **heard** that voice **calling** his name again. "Samuel! Samuel!"
"Speak, Lord. I'm **listening**!" Samuel said.
Eli was right! GOD had been **calling** Samuel's name!
Samuel **listened** carefully to all God had to tell him.
He did his best to remember everything God said!
God's words are IMPORTANT.

For older children: How many ears can you find on this page?

Samuel Obeys God

1 Samuel 16:1-13

Help your child point to the person telling his part of the story.

I'm Samuel.

I love God. When I was a boy, I learned to obey God.

One day when I was grown up, God told me to visit a man named Jesse.

"I have chosen one of Jesse's sons to be the new king," God said.

So I obeyed God. I went to see Jesse.

I'm Jesse.

Samuel came to see me.

He told me God had chosen one of my sons to be the new king.

I called my sons together.

Samuel met the oldest one, tall and handsome. Samuel looked at him.

Then he shook his head no and met my second son.

He shook his head no again. Samuel met seven of my sons.

He kept shaking his head no.

Samuel asked, "Do you have any more sons?"

I told him, "I have one more young son, David.

He is out taking care of the sheep."

Samuel asked me to bring David to meet him.

I'm David.

I was out with the sheep. I heard footsteps running toward me.

"David!" my brother called. "Come home!"

So I obeyed. I came right back to the house.

There was Samuel. "This is the one!" Samuel said.

Samuel put a little oil on my head.

He told my family that God had chosen me to be the new king.

WOW! I was surprised! But I love God.

So I will obey!

Samuel obeyed God, and I will, too.

For older children: How many sheep are hiding on this page?

42

David Helps His Family

1 Samuel 16:11-12,18; 17:34-35

Once there lived a little boy with seven bigger brothers.

Though was growing every day, he was smaller than the others.

 was the youngest. But one day his father said,

"You're big enough to tend our  and make sure they're fed."

So went to tend the sheep. He walked beside his .

Some  ran and skipped with him. Some climbed up on the .

In the quiet afternoon, when lay in the shade,

 watched for  and . He was not afraid!

If any or  came to steal a lamb,

David chased them, stopped them and took back his lamb again!

If a  was sick or hurt, David took good care.

He carried that poor on his shoulders everywhere.

While the were eating, standing in the sun,

 played his and sang. It was lots of fun!

 loved to sing to God. He loved to let God know that

he loved God and showed God's love by helping his grow!

David   sheep   flock   rocks

bears   lions   harp

Point to the pictures and let your child help you read the story.

For older children: Find the hidden lion and bear.

43

David Visits His Brothers

Help your child count on fingers whenever you say a number.

1 Samuel 17:12-20

Father Jesse had eight sons. (1,2,3,4,5,6,7,8)
But three sons left home one day. (1,2,3)
They joined their country's army to chase enemies away.

David was the youngest son,
The one who stayed at home to watch the sheep. (1)
Every day, he found good grass and cool shade where
  they could sleep.

He led the sheep to quiet water,
  and made sure they had a drink.
At night, David kept them safe and counted them
  so carefully I think.

Father Jesse wondered, *Do my three sons need food?*
  (1,2,3)
My sons have gone so far away.
I wonder if they're safe and have a place to stay?

Father Jesse worried.
"David, please go find them," Father Jesse said.
"Pack up your donkeys and take some grain and
  cheese and bread."

David loaded up his donkeys,
Maybe one or two or three. (1,2,3)
Then he started off across the hills as far as he could see.

He tied bags to the donkey's backs;
He tied on baskets full of grain and bread.
He wanted to help his brothers, just like his father said.

Finally David saw the camp
And soon he found his brothers.
He gave them all the food he'd brought; he knew
  they'd share with others.

David was glad to help his family.
He showed love by doing good!
Three bags and six baskets—what a lot of tasty
  food! (1,2,3,4,5,6)

For older children: Count aloud as high as you can!

David and Jonathan Are Kind

1 Samuel 16:15-23; 18:1-4; 19:1-7

*Each time you say the word **friend**,
give a high five to your child.*

King Saul had gotten grumpy. He wasn't making any **friends**!

So King Saul's servants sent for a harp player.

"Maybe music will HELP the grumpy king!" they said.

The harp player was David! And his playing DID help King Saul feel happy again.

King Saul's son was named Jonathan. He became David's best **friend**.

They probably shot arrows together. They walked and talked together.

Maybe the **friends** played music and sang together!

One day, these **friends** made a promise to each other:

They would ALWAYS be **friends**, no matter what!

Jonathan also gave David some special gifts.

He gave David his own coat. He gave David his own bow and arrow.

He gave these gifts to show that David was his best **friend**.

Later, King Saul got VERY angry and grumpy. He wanted to HURT David!

Jonathan helped his **friend** David get away to a safe place.

He talked to King Saul. He made sure it was safe for David to come back.

The **friends** must have been very glad to be together again!

For older children: How many arrows can you find hidden in the pictures?

45

David and Saul

1 Samuel 26

Make the motions and encourage your child to imitate them.

King Saul was very angry. **Shake fist**.

He did NOT want David to be king. **Shake head no**.

David and his friends were hiding in some caves and rocky hills. **Cover head**.

King Saul brought his army to look for them.

When it got dark, King Saul and his army went to sleep. **Rest head on hands**.

David and a friend tiptoed to the place where Saul was sleeping. **"Shh!"**

David's friend wanted to hurt King Saul.

But David said, "NO!" **Shake head no**.

He would not hurt King Saul, no matter what!

David and his friend took the king's spear and water jug. **Pretend to carry both**.

They carried King Saul's things to the top of the hill.

When they were on the hilltop, David called out. **Cup hands around mouth**.

"King Saul, where is your water jug? Where is your spear?"

King Saul jumped up.

He could see that David held up the king's own jug and spear.

The king called back, "Is that you, David?" **Cup hands around mouth**.

David said, "I could have hurt you. But I did not." **Shake head no**.

King Saul said, "I was wrong! I will not try to hurt you.

May God take care of you."

God had helped David to be kind to Saul, even though Saul had not been kind to David. **Nod head yes**.

For older children:
How many things can you find that rhyme with the word "jug"?

46

David and Mephibosheth

1 Samuel 20:14-17,42;
2 Samuel 9

*Every time you say
a person's name, ask
your child to wiggle
his or her toes!*

David and **Jonathan** had been very best friends.
They had promised to always help each other.
They had promised to help each other's families, too.
Now **David** had become king. **Jonathan** had died in a war.

But **David** never forgot his friend. He never forgot his promise.
He asked, "Is anyone still living who is part of **Jonathan's** family?
I would like to be kind and help!"
So **David's** servants told him about **Mephibosheth**.

Mephibosheth was **Jonathan's** son. His feet had been hurt.
He couldn't walk easily. **David** wanted to help!
King **David** sent servants to Mephibosheth's house.
The servants told **Mephibosheth** the king wanted to see him.
When **Mephibosheth** came to the palace, he bowed very low.

David said, "**Mephibosheth**, I want you and your family to
    come and live with me. I want you to eat with me.
I will treat you as if you were my own son."
David helped **Mephibosheth**.
He was kind to **Mephibosheth** and his family!

For older children: How many circles can you find on
the page? How many rectangles?

Birds Feed Elijah

Invite your child to nod or shake head as you read the story.

1 Kings 17:1-6

Elijah was God's helper. He told people God's words. **Nod.**

One day God told Elijah, "No rain will fall for a long, long time." **Shake head no.**

No rain? Then no food could grow! **Shake head no.**

And if no food grew, EVERYONE was going to be hungry! **Nod.**

"I will take care of you," God told Elijah. **Nod.**

God said, "Go and live by a little stream of water called Kerith. I will make the birds bring food to you." **Nod.**

Elijah did just as God said. He walked up and down the dry hills. He saw no clouds in the sky! **Shake head no.**

Finally, Elijah came to the little stream God had told him about. He drank cool water from the stream. Now he felt better! **Nod.**

Elijah looked around. The plants and trees nearby were dry and brown. No food was growing here! And Elijah had no food with him. **Shake head no.**

So Elijah waited. He remembered that God had promised to take care of him. **Nod.**

Soon Elijah saw ravens! The big black birds flew nearer and nearer. Some carried bread. Others carried meat. They dropped the food and then they flew away. **Nod.**

Elijah didn't need to worry! **Shake head no.**

God sent the ravens with food, every night and every morning! God loved and took care of Elijah. **Nod.**

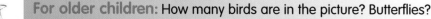

For older children: How many birds are in the picture? Butterflies?

God Cares for a Widow

1 Kings 17:7-16

God had told me there would be no more rain.
God sent me to live beside a stream and sent birds with bread and meat.
But then the stream dried up! Then God told me to go to a town.
He said a woman there would have food. So that's where I went!

I picked up some sticks so that I could bake our last bit of bread,
 just enough for my son and me.
But this man Elijah asked me to bring him a drink of water.
Then he asked me for some bread, too! I told him, "I only have
 enough flour and oil to make bread for my son and myself.
That will be our last food."

I told her not to be afraid. I told her to make a little bread for me first.
God had promised me that there would be enough food for all of us!

I mixed some flour and oil. I patted out my bread.
After it baked, I gave it to Elijah.
Then I went to see if there was any flour in the flour jar.
I was AMAZED! There was more flour!
I peeked into the oil pitcher. There was MORE oil!
I had enough flour and oil to make all the bread we needed!

And every day after that, we had enough flour and oil.
We had plenty of bread! Thank You, God!

For older children: How many circles can you find in this picture? Triangles?

Elisha's New Room

2 Kings 4:8-10

Do the motions as you read.
Invite your child to imitate you.

Elisha walked many places to tell people about God. **Walk fingers.**

In one town, Elisha stopped. **Stop walking fingers.**

A kind lady and her husband lived in this town.
This lady often listened to Elisha talk about God. **Cup hand behind ear.**

One day the kind lady asked Elisha to eat dinner with them.
After that, Elisha ate with them every time he came to town. **Pretend to eat.**

Then Elisha would walk on to the next town. **Walk fingers.**

One day the woman said to her husband, "Elisha obeys and loves God.
I want to do something kind for him." **Nod.**

"Let's build a room for him on the flat roof of our house.
We'll put a chair and a table and a lamp and a bed in the room.
Whenever Elisha comes to visit, he can sleep in his own room." **Pretend to sleep.**

The woman's husband thought it was a good idea. **Nod.**

So they began to build a room for Elisha. They sawed wood. **Pretend to saw.**

They pounded with hammers. **Pretend to hammer.**

They worked until Elisha's room was built on the flat roof.
They moved a chair, table, lamp and bed into the room. **Count on fingers.**

It was just right! They could hardly wait until Elisha came back. **Smile.**

One day Elisha came to town. When he got to the woman's house, she said,
   "Come quickly, Elisha. We have something special to show you!" **Beckon.**

The woman and her husband walked Elisha up the stairs to the roof of their house.
There was his new room! Elisha must have been surprised! **Look surprised.**

Elisha was glad God cared for him by giving him kind friends.
Now he could sleep in his very own room! **Pretend to sleep.**

For older children: Find items that begin with the "B" sound in the picture.

God Helps Naaman

Invite your child to hold up the appropriate number of fingers when you read numbers in the story.

2 Kings 5:1-16

One army commander named Naaman
Was sick as sick could be.
He had painful sores all over.
He was sick with leprosy.

But **one** servant girl from Israel
Knew God had power to help.
She was sure Elisha could ask God
To make her master well!

So the servant girl told Naaman's wife.
His wife told Naaman the news.
Naaman told his king. The king wrote a letter
And sent gifts for Naaman to use.

Naaman went to see Israel's king.
The king didn't understand.
He said, "I'm not God! I don't make
People well. I can't help this man!"

But Elisha heard of Naaman's visit and said
"Send Naaman down to me."
So Naaman went to Elisha's door.
But Elisha he did not see!

Elisha's servant told him,
"Wash in this river **seven** times.
Then your skin will all be healed.
You'll be feeling fine."

Naaman got angry. What a silly idea!
He started to walk away.
But Naaman's servant stopped him.
He said Naaman should obey!

So Naaman walked to the river.
He went in and ducked his head.
One, two, three, four, five, six, seven times,
Under the water he went!

Naaman came up dripping.
Naaman looked to see.
His sores were gone! Naaman said,
"The **one** true God healed me!"

God's great power helped Naaman.
God will help us, too.
He loves us and cares for us.
He does what He says He will do!

For older children: Count the numbers in the story.

51

Joash Repairs the Temple

Do the actions indicated as you read. Invite your child to imitate you.

2 Kings 12:4-15; 2 Chronicles 24:1-14

God's Temple once was beautiful. People came to pray to God.
Fold hands as though praying.
But after many years, people forgot about God.
No one came to the Temple. **Shake head no.**
It was dirty! It was dusty! Sneeze.
The golden bowls and candlesticks were stolen. Shake finger.
The walls were broken. But nobody cared. Nobody came. Shake head no.

One day Joash became king. **Put on imaginary crown.**
He was seven years old. He loved God! **Clap hands as though cheering.**
When Joash grew up, he saw how broken and dirty God's Temple had become.
He wanted God's people to love God and obey Him again. **Nod.**

So King Joash planned to make the Temple beautiful once more.
He would need many helpers. It would take a lot of work! **Flex arm.**
And it would take a lot of money!
So Joash told the Temple helpers to tell God's people,
Hands to mouth like a megaphone.
"We need EVERYONE to help make the Temple beautiful. Spread arms out.
Please help by bringing money to the big box at the Temple."
Clink! Clink! Clink! The money boxes got full. **Drop imaginary coins in box.**

The helpers' saws began to zoom, zoom, zoom. **Pretend to saw.**
The helpers' hammers went tap, tap, tap. **Pretend to hammer.**
Some helpers dusted. Some swept the floor. Pretend to sweep.
Some helpers made new bowls and vases and candlesticks.
When they were done, the Temple was clean and beautiful again.
Clap hands as though cheering.
King Joash called God's people to come to the Temple. **Beckon.**
The people were glad to pray to God again in the beautiful Temple!
Fold hands as though praying.

For older children: Find the items in the picture whose names begin with the "B," "C," "D," "K" and "S" sounds?

Josiah Reads God's Words

2 Chronicles 34—35:19

Josiah was a little boy.
He was only eight years old.
They put a crown upon his head.
The crown was made of **gold**.

Josiah then became the king.
He wanted to obey.
He wanted to do what was good
Every night and **day**.

But Josiah and his people
Had no scroll of God's Word.
They could not learn about the Lord.
God's Word they'd never **heard**!

Josiah told his workers,
"Let's make God's Temple clean!"
When they swept, they found God's scroll.
What could the scroll's words **mean**?

A servant put the dusty scroll
In King Josiah's hand.
Josiah read it and then he learned
How he should rule his **land**.

Josiah sent this order out:
"The people, every one,
Must come to hear the scroll be read
To find out what should be **done**."

King Josiah read the scroll.
He promised to obey.
His people said they'd obey too,
Every single **day**!

God's people then obeyed
    God's Word.
They did what was right.
They prayed and sang and
    worshiped God
For many days and **nights**!

For older children: How many words can you think of that rhyme with the word "king"?
With the word "scroll"? With the word "crown"?

Nehemiah Helps Build Walls

Nehemiah 1—2; 4:1-6; 6:15-16; 12:27,43

Invite your child to name the pictures as you read the rebus story.

Nehemiah   walls   King   prayed

Jerusalem   God's people

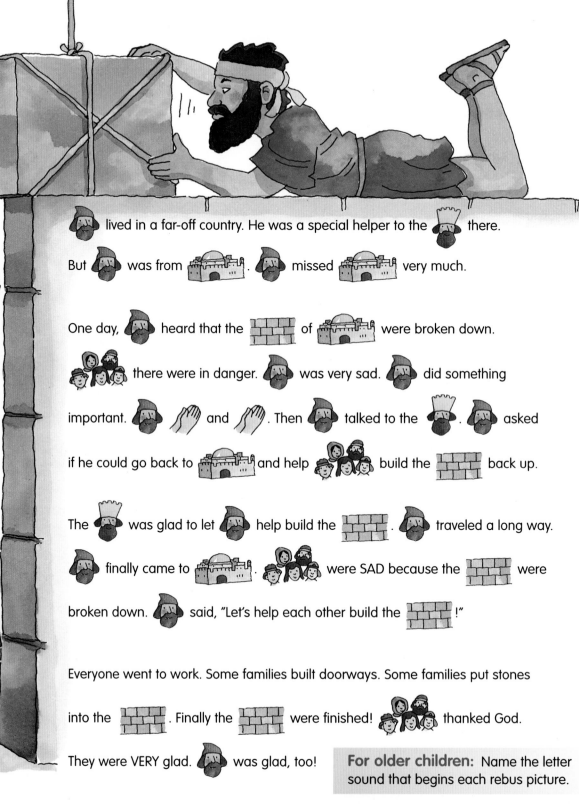

[Nehemiah] lived in a far-off country. He was a special helper to the [King] there.

But [Nehemiah] was from [Jerusalem]. [Nehemiah] missed [Jerusalem] very much.

One day, [Nehemiah] heard that the [walls] of [Jerusalem] were broken down. [God's people] there were in danger. [Nehemiah] was very sad. [Nehemiah] did something important. [Nehemiah] [prayed] and [prayed]. Then [Nehemiah] talked to the [King]. [Nehemiah] asked if he could go back to [Jerusalem] and help [God's people] build the [walls] back up.

The [King] was glad to let [Nehemiah] help build the [walls]. [Nehemiah] traveled a long way. [Nehemiah] finally came to [Jerusalem]. [God's people] were SAD because the [walls] were broken down. [Nehemiah] said, "Let's help each other build the [walls]!"

Everyone went to work. Some families built doorways. Some families put stones into the [walls]. Finally the [walls] were finished! [God's people] thanked God.

They were VERY glad. [Nehemiah] was glad, too!

For older children: Name the letter sound that begins each rebus picture.

54

Esther Is Brave

Esther 2—9

Point to the pictures and let your child help you read the story.

Esther   Mordecai   King Xerxes   palace   Haman   law

[Esther] was a beautiful young woman. Her cousin [Mordecai] had raised [Esther].

One day [King Xerxes] (ZUHRK-sees) chose [Esther] to be his queen and live in the [palace]! [King Xerxes] gave [Esther] beautiful clothes and jewelry.

[King Xerxes] had a helper named [Haman]. [Haman] wanted to kill Esther's cousin [Mordecai] and ALL of Mordecai's people—everyone who was a Jew. [King Xerxes] did not know [Esther] was a Jew. [Haman] tricked [King Xerxes] into making a [law] to kill all the Jews.

[Mordecai] told [Esther] about [Haman]'s [law]. [Esther] wanted to ask [King Xerxes] to stop this bad [law]! But anyone who came to [King Xerxes] without being asked could be killed—even the queen!

[Esther] said, "I will talk to [King Xerxes], even though I am afraid." For three days, [Esther], [Mordecai], and all the other Jews prayed and did not eat anything. Then [Esther] put on her beautiful jewelry and clothes.

She stood at the door of the room in the [palace] where [King Xerxes] sat. When [King Xerxes] saw [Esther], he was glad to see her!

Later at a dinner for [King Xerxes] and [Haman], [Esther] told [King Xerxes] that someone was going to KILL her people. [Esther] asked [King Xerxes] to please save her life and the lives of all her people. [King Xerxes] asked, "Who would DO such a terrible thing?"

[Esther] pointed. "The man who is doing this is [Haman]!" [King Xerxes] had [Haman] taken away! Then [King Xerxes] wrote a new [law] to protect the Jews.

[Esther] and [Mordecai] and all God's people were VERY happy!

For older children: Find the crowns in the picture. Some are hidden!

Jeremiah Obeys

Invite your child to say the repeating word with you.

Jeremiah 36

Jeremiah told the people God's Word, Word, Word.
The people didn't like what they heard, heard, heard.
They were doing wrong day and **night, night, night**.
That's why God told Jeremiah what to write, write, write.

So Jeremiah said God's words and then, then, then
Baruch his helper wrote them with a **pen, pen, pen**.
When Jeremiah had said every **word, word, word**,
Baruch knew these words had to be **heard, heard, heard**.

Baruch read the scroll in a voice so **loud, loud, loud**
That everyone could hear him in the **crowd, crowd, crowd**.
The people heard God's words being read, read, read.
Some people didn't like what God had said, said, said.

People told the king what they had heard, heard, heard.
They told him how Baruch read every word, word, word.
The king didn't LIKE what God had said, said, said!
He took the scroll and burned it up instead, instead, instead!

The king sliced up the scroll, burned it to ash, ash, ash!
He thought God's words were gone and in the **trash, trash, trash**!
But God told Jeremiah, "Take your **pen, pen, pen**.
It's time to write down My words **again, again, again**."

Jeremiah and Baruch obeyed the Lord, Lord, Lord.
They wrote on a new scroll all of God's Word, Word, Word.
The people did not listen and obey, obey, obey,
But Baruch and Jeremiah did—each day, day, day!

For older children: Find the following objects: cat, bird, pen, umbrella. Some of them are hidden.

Daniel Obeys God

Daniel 1

Do the motions indicated. Invite your child to imitate you.

The king of Babylon marched to Jerusalem. **March feet**.

He marched many people from Jerusalem back to Babylon with him. **March feet**.

Four boys came from Israel—Daniel and his 3 friends. Hold up 4 fingers.

The king's helper pointed to these boys. **Point**.

He said, "You will be trained to work for the king.

You can only eat food from the king's table." **Nod**.

Daniel and his 3 friends shook their heads. **Shake head no**.

God had told His people not to eat those foods. Pretend to push food away.

Daniel and his friends decided they were going to obey God! **Nod**.

But the king's helper said they HAD to eat the king's food. **Shake finger**.

Daniel and his friends knew they HAD to obey God! **Nod**.

So Daniel asked the guard in charge of meals to give them only vegetables and water for 10 days. Hold up 10 fingers.

For 10 days, Daniel and his friends ate only vegetables. **Pretend to eat**.

They drank only water. **Pretend to drink**.

After 10 days, the guard looked at the 4 boys. Hold up 4 fingers.

Daniel and his friends looked healthier and stronger than anyone else did! **Flex muscle**.

So the guard said they did not have to eat the king's food. **Nod**.

They were glad they had obeyed God! **Clap**.

For older children: Count the circles and triangles in the picture.

57

The Fiery Furnace

Daniel 3

Invite your child to read the story with you, naming the rebus pictures.

3 friends   **king**   **statue**   **furnace**   **bow**

Daniel had [3 friends]. They lived in Babylon and worked for the [king]. The [king] made a BIG golden [statue]. The [king] made this rule: "When the music plays, [bow] down. PRAY to this [statue]. If you do not [bow], you will be thrown in a [furnace] to be BURNED UP!" When the music began to play, people began to [bow] and pray to the [statue]. But the [3 friends] stood tall. They would ONLY pray to God! The [king] heard the [3 friends] would not [bow] to his statue. He was ANGRY! He roared at the [3 friends], "[bow] NOW or you'll be thrown into the [furnace]. Who will help you THEN?"

The [3 friends] said, "Our God can save us from the [furnace]. Even if He doesn't, we won't [bow] to your [statue]!" NOW the [king] was REALLY angry! He ordered that the [furnace] be made hotter. Soldiers tied the [3 friends] up and threw them into the HOTTEST part of the [furnace]. "Look!" said the [king]." "Didn't we throw in [3 friends]? There are 4 now. They are not tied up anymore!" God had sent an angel into the hot [furnace] to keep the [3 friends] safe! The [king] ordered the [3 friends] to come out of the [furnace]. They DID! They were not burned at ALL. The [king] praised the one true God! He said, "No one may say anything bad about the God of these [3 friends]!" The [3 friends] trusted God. And God took care of them!

For older children: Circle the word "God" in the story.

58

The Writing on the Wall

King Belshazzar was king of Babylon. He liked parties. One night he had a big dinner for his friends.

The king and his friends drank from the golden cups from God's Temple. No one cared that the cups belonged to God. The king did not love and obey God.

Suddenly, a HAND appeared! It began to write words on the wall! Everyone was very quiet. King Belshazzar was very afraid.

The words stayed on the wall. And the king's helpers could not tell what the words meant. The king was even MORE afraid!

The queen told the king to call for Daniel. He could tell what the words meant. Daniel came. He DID know what the words meant.

The words meant that God knew Belshazzar had not loved and obeyed God. His time as king was now OVER. Another king would take his place.

And it happened just as God said. ANOTHER king came in and took over that VERY night! Daniel was asked to work for the new king.

For older children: How many hands can you count?

59

The Lions' Den

Daniel 6

Daniel prayed three times a day.
Everybody knew
That Daniel loved the Lord his God
And pray is what he'd do.

But the king made one new law.
"You must pray to ME.
If you don't, the lion's den
Is where you're going to be!"

But Daniel prayed to God alone.
So three times that day
He knelt down and gave thanks.
He knew he should pray.

The king soon heard from other men
That Daniel prayed each day.
And Daniel soon was sent to spend
The night where lions stay!

Daniel prayed to God again.
God sent help, all right.
An angel shut those lions' mouths,
Daniel was safe all night!

For older children: Which lion is biggest? Which lion is smallest? What makes one lion different from the others?

60

Jonah and the Big Fish

Do the suggested actions. Invite your child to join you.

Jonah

I'm Jonah. I tell people messages from God. **Point to self**.

One day God told me, "Go to Nineveh." **Point away**. "Tell those people to stop doing wrong."

Now I did not like the people of Nineveh. **Frown**.

So I did NOT go to Nineveh. **Shake head no**. I did NOT want to obey God.

I got onto a ship going far away from Nineveh. Down in the big ship, I went to sleep. **Pretend to sleep**.

That's when God sent a STORM. The waves CRASHED. The water SPLASHED.

The sailors were AFRAID! But I was still ASLEEP. The sailors shook me and woke me. They wanted me to PRAY! But I knew God had sent the storm because I had not obeyed. **Nod**. So I said, "Throw me in the water. Then the storm will STOP."

So one, two, THREE! **Count on fingers**. The sailors threw me in. SPLASH!

The storm STOPPED. But I sank like a stone. Down, down, DOWN! Suddenly, a HUGE fish swam by. **Wiggle hands like a fish**.

It opened its mouth WIDE and WHOOSH! I was in the big fish's BELLY! **Pat belly**.

I began to PRAY. **Bow head and fold hands**.

I asked God to forgive me. I promised to obey. I would go to Nineveh to tell God's message. I prayed and WAITED.

God sent that big fish close to the land of Nineveh, right up to the beach. That fish coughed and choked and coughed me up! I crawled onto the beach. **Pretend to crawl**. God talked to me again. **Cup hand behind ear**.

God said, "Go! Tell those people in Nineveh that they have disobeyed Me!"

This time I OBEYED! **Nod**. I went to Nineveh. I told everyone they had not obeyed God. And the people LISTENED. They asked God to forgive them for doing wrong things. And God did!

For older children: How many fish have three fins? Four fins? How many have no fins at all?

New Testament

Mary Hears Good News

Point to the pictures and let your child help you read the story.

promise   Mary   baby   Elizabeth   Joseph

Matthew 1:18-25; Luke 1:26-56

A long time ago, God told His people a _promise_ .

God said He would send His Son to live with His people on Earth.

His Son would be the Savior.

But God did not say when He would send His Son.

So God's people waited and waited.

When would God keep His _promise_ to send His Son?

God was about to make His _promise_ come true.

One day God sent an angel to visit a young woman named _Mary_ .

The angel surprised _Mary_ . She was afraid!

The angel said, "Don't be afraid, _Mary_ . God loves you.

God has chosen you to be the mother of the most special _baby_ ever born.

Name the _baby_, Jesus. He will be God's own Son.

He will be the Savior."

Mary wanted to share her good news!

So she went to see her cousin _Elizabeth_ .

God told _Elizabeth_ that _Mary_ was going to be the mother of His Son, Jesus.

Elizabeth was glad to see _Mary_ .

She and _Mary_ praised God together!

There was one other person the angel visited!

A man named _Joseph_ was going to be Mary's husband.

While he slept, an angel talked to him in a dream.

The angel told _Joseph_ that _Mary_ was going to have a special _baby_.

The angel told _Joseph_ to name the _baby_ Jesus.

Joseph must have been excited!

Now God's _promise_ made so long ago was going to come true!

For older children: Which face in the story looks afraid? Happy? Sleepy?

John Is Born

Read the story and then sing it to the tune of the "ABC Song" with your child.

Luke 1:5-25,57-80

Here's a story that's often told.
A man and his wife were both very old.
They had no daughter. They had no son.
They had no children, not even one.
God's plan for Zechariah and Elizabeth was wise.
He planned to send them a son—surprise!
One day, Zechariah was in the Temple.
He looked up to see an angel!

The angel said, "You will have a son!
He'll do God's work. You will name him John."
Zechariah asked, "How can I know it's true?"
The angel said, "GOD sent me to you!
Since you don't believe, you won't be heard.
Until John is born, you can't say a word!"
Elizabeth knew that God had done
A wonderful thing, giving them a son.

Family and friends came to see the baby boy.
They all were glad. They were full of joy!
They all guessed what his name would be.
They said, "Zechariah, just like his daddy."
Elizabeth said, "No! His name is John."
Zechariah found something to write his name on.
Zechariah wrote: "John is his name!"
He began to speak and out the words came!

Zechariah prayed and he thanked God!
He told about John's important job.
He said, "God has a plan that He will show.
God will keep great promises He made long ago.
God's Savior will love people big and small.
John will tell of this Savior to one and all."
Zechariah could talk; Zechariah could sing!
Elizabeth and he praised God for everything.

For older children: Point to each name you find in the story.
Count how many times you see each name.

Baby Jesus

As you read, say the word "**surprise**" loudly.
Invite your child to imitate you.

Luke 1:26-33; 2:1-7

Mary was all by herself. When she looked up, **surprise**!

An angel was standing right in front of her!

The angel said, "Hello! God loves you, Mary."

Surprise again! Mary's eyes grew wide.

The angel said, "Don't be afraid. God is pleased with you.

You will be the mother of the MOST special baby ever born.

Name Him Jesus."

This baby was not even born yet. But, **surprise**!

He already had a name!

She told the angel, "I am ready to do what God wants."

Later on, Mary and Joseph had another **surprise**!

The king said they had to go to a town far away.

So they walked and walked to the town of Bethlehem.

They looked for a place to sleep.

But **surprise**! There was no room in any place they asked to stay.

Surprise! A man said they could sleep in the stable.

A stable was the place where the animals slept and ate.

Surprise! Mary and Joseph slept in the stable.

While they were there, there came the BIGGEST, BEST **SURPRISE**!

Mary's baby was born! She and Joseph named Him Jesus, as the angel said.

They wrapped baby Jesus in soft cloths to keep Him warm. They rocked Him.

Where would He sleep? They wondered. **Surprise**!

They laid baby Jesus in the manger, the trough where the animals ate their hay.

Surprise! The animals that came to eat found a BABY in the hay!

Mary had a **surprise**. Joseph had a **surprise**. The animals had a **surprise**.

And soon the whole world would know about God's wonderful **SURPRISE**!

For older children: Tell the sound of the letter that begins the name of each animal in the picture.

66

Jesus Is Born

Make the motions and encourage your child to imitate you.

Luke 2:1-7

It was almost time for Mary's baby to be born.
Mary must have been glad! **Smile.**

Joseph told Mary, "The king says we must go to Bethlehem.

We must write our names in the king's book." **Pretend to write.**

Mary and Joseph packed their things. **Pretend to pack a bag.**

They started on their trip to Bethlehem. **Pretend to pick up and carry a bag.**

Mary and Joseph walked and walked. Mary may have ridden on a donkey.
Walk fingers.

They stopped by the road and slept. **Pillow head on hands.**

When morning came, they got up and traveled again! **Walk fingers.**

Finally, Mary and Joseph came to the city of Bethlehem.

The city was FULL of people. **Nod.**

They had all come to write their names in the king's book, too!
Pretend to write.

Joseph looked for a place where they could sleep. **Look around.**

Joseph and Mary knocked on the door of an inn,
a place like a big house for many people. **Knock.**

There was no room there. **Shake head no.**

But the innkeeper said, "Wait! You can sleep out in the stable."

Sheep and cows and donkeys were sleeping there,
but that was fine.

Joseph and Mary were tired! **Yawn.**

They were glad for a place to lie down and rest!
Pillow head on hands.

That very night, in that very stable, God's promise came true!
Nod.

Jesus was born! Mary wrapped Him and rocked Him.
Pretend to rock baby.

Mary lay baby Jesus down to sleep in the manger,
the place where the animals eat. **Pretend to lay baby down.**

Mary and Joseph were VERY glad baby Jesus was born!

For older children: How many animals can you count? How many stars?

Angels Tell the News

Speak very softly as you read sentences in blue.
Speak louder as you read sentences in red.

Luke 2:8-20

It was a quiet night. Tiny stars twinkled high in the sky.
Sheep and little lambs lay sleeping together.
Some sleepy shepherds sat by their fire.
They could hear the quiet sounds of their sheep.

Suddenly, it got as bright as daytime!
The shepherds looked at each other with big eyes.
What was happening?
They looked up. There in front of them was an ANGEL!

The angel said, "Don't be afraid!
I have GOOD NEWS to tell everyone.
Tonight in Bethlehem, JESUS, the Savior, was born!
You can see Him! He is wrapped in cloth.
He is lying in a manger!"
Then it got even BRIGHTER!
The whole sky filled with angels!
The angels said, "GLORY TO GOD IN THE HIGHEST!"

Then the angels were gone.
It was very quiet and dark again.
The shepherds looked at each other.
"Let's GO!" they said to each other.
"Let's go to Bethlehem and see this baby!"
They must have started RUNNING!

The shepherds came to a stable.
Inside, they could see a newborn baby.
He was lying in a manger!
They tiptoed inside.
Here was Jesus, just as the angel had said!
They were glad and quietly thanked God!
Then the shepherds tiptoed out.

When the shepherds went outside,
They used their outside voices!
They began to tell EVERYONE they saw,
"Listen, everyone! We have GOOD NEWS!
Jesus is born! GOOD NEWS!"

For older children: How many things in the picture can you find that begin with an "S" sound?

Shepherds at the Stable

Luke 2:8-20

Point to each picture and invite your child to tell the story with you.

For older children: Find the circles and triangles in the pictures.

Wise Men Give Gifts

Matthew 2:1-12

Follow the path to read the story. Invite your child to trace the path with a finger.

There were some men who lived far away from Bethlehem. They were called wise men because they knew many things. God wanted these men to know Jesus had been born.

These men looked at the stars often. One night, they were surprised to see a new star! The new star was VERY bright! The wise men believed it meant a great new king had been born! They decided to follow that star to find the new king.

Finally the wise men came to a big city. There they talked to the king of that city. They asked, "Where is the new king who was born? We have seen His star. We have come here to give Him gifts."

The wise men packed up for a VERY long trip. They also packed up special gifts for the new king. They loaded their camels. They traveled for many days.

The king was surprised. He did not know about any new king! His teachers told him that God had promised to send a King to be born in Bethlehem. The wise men were glad to know this. They went right to Bethlehem!

The star they had followed stopped right over one house. The wise men got their gifts and went to the house. They knocked on the door and went in. They saw little Jesus and knelt down.

The wise men gave their gifts to Jesus to show they loved Him. They gave Him gold and incense and perfume. These were special gifts for the King they had come to see—Jesus! The wise men were glad God had led them with the star!

For older children: How many rocks can you count along the road?

Escape to Egypt

Matthew 2:1-15

shining   riding   looking   walking

When you read the words below, do the actions shown. Invite your child to join you.

After Jesus was born in Bethlehem, God wanted some people to know this good news! So God put a bright **shining** star in the sky. The **shining** star told people that a new King was born. Some wise men who lived far away saw the **shining** star.

"Let's find this King!" they said. "We'll take gifts to this King." The wise men packed their camels and began **riding**. After **riding** for days and days, they were finally **riding** into Jerusalem. At King Herod's palace they said, "We are **looking** for the new King. We want to worship Him."

King Herod did not know about this new King. HE wanted to be the ONLY king! King Herod found out where Jesus was to be born. He told the wise men, "Keep **looking** for the child. When you find Him, tell me. I want to worship Him, too." But King Herod lied. He REALLY wanted to KILL Jesus!

The wise men went **riding** away. They followed the **shining** star right to the house where Jesus was! When the wise men saw Jesus, they bowed low. They gave Him their gifts. Here was the great King they had been **looking** for!

The wise men might have gone back to tell King Herod where Jesus was, but God told them, "Do NOT go back to King Herod." So away they went, **riding** back home by another road. They never told King Herod!

After the wise men went **riding** away, an angel talked to Joseph in a dream. "Get up," the angel said. "King Herod wants to hurt Jesus. Take Mary and Jesus to Egypt." Joseph woke Mary. "We must start **walking** now," Joseph said. "An angel told me to take you and Jesus to Egypt."

Mary and Joseph picked up Jesus. They started **walking** quietly and quickly so that no one would notice them. After many days of **walking**, they were in Egypt! Joseph and Mary and Jesus were safe! God was with Joseph and Mary. He helped them keep Jesus safe. And God is with us, too!

For older children: Think of some actions to do. Let your family guess what you are acting out!

Jesus at the Temple

Follow the path with your finger to read the story. Invite your child to join you.

Matthew 2:19-23;
Luke 2:41-52

Jesus was a baby once. He grew and grew and grew.
He learned to talk and learned to walk, just the same as you!

Joseph was a carpenter. He made things out of wood.
Jesus learned from Joseph how to make things that were good.

They made chairs and stools, some tables and some toys.
Jesus grew and Jesus learned. His parents loved their boy!

The days went by; the years went past. Jesus kept on growing.
One day to Jerusalem His family was going.

They traveled to the Temple to worship, sing and pray.
His family loved to worship God and stayed for seven days!

When it was time to go back home, the families started walking.
The moms and dads, the boys and girls were very busy talking.

But when time came for everyone to stop and sleep at night,
Mary and Joseph looked for Jesus, but He was not in sight.

Jesus' family looked for Him. They went throughout the town.
They went back to the Temple and there Jesus was found.

He wasn't scared; He wasn't sad. He knew God's love that day.
God's love is great for all of us, no matter where we stay!

For older children: How many sheep can you count? How many donkeys?

John Preaches in the Desert

Matthew 3:1-6;
Mark 1:1-8;
Luke 3:1-18

Out there in the desert, it was dry and hot.

Look for John in the desert.

John lived in the desert by himself.

John wore rough clothes made from camel's hair.

He ate the **insects** and the sweet honey he found there.

Look for John near the Jordan River.

People came to the river to listen to John.

John told the people, "Get ready for the Savior God promised to send!"

Men, women and **children** listened to John.

John told people to stop doing wrong and do what is right.

People asked, "What should we do?"

John said, "If you have two **coats**, give one **coat** to a person
  who has no **coat**.

If you have extra **food**, give some to hungry people."

Some **soldiers** came to listen, too.

John told them, "Don't take money that doesn't belong to you.

Tell other people only what is true."

Many people wanted to stop doing wrong things and start
  doing good things.

They asked John to baptize them.

See the **river**? John baptized the people in the **river**.

He used the water to show that God washes away the wrong
  things they have done.

For older children: How many insects do you see in the
desert picture? How many fish do you see in the river?

John Baptizes Jesus

**Matthew 3:13-17; Mark 1:9-11;
Luke 3:21-22; John 1:29-34**

Invite your child to point to the pictures and read the story with you.

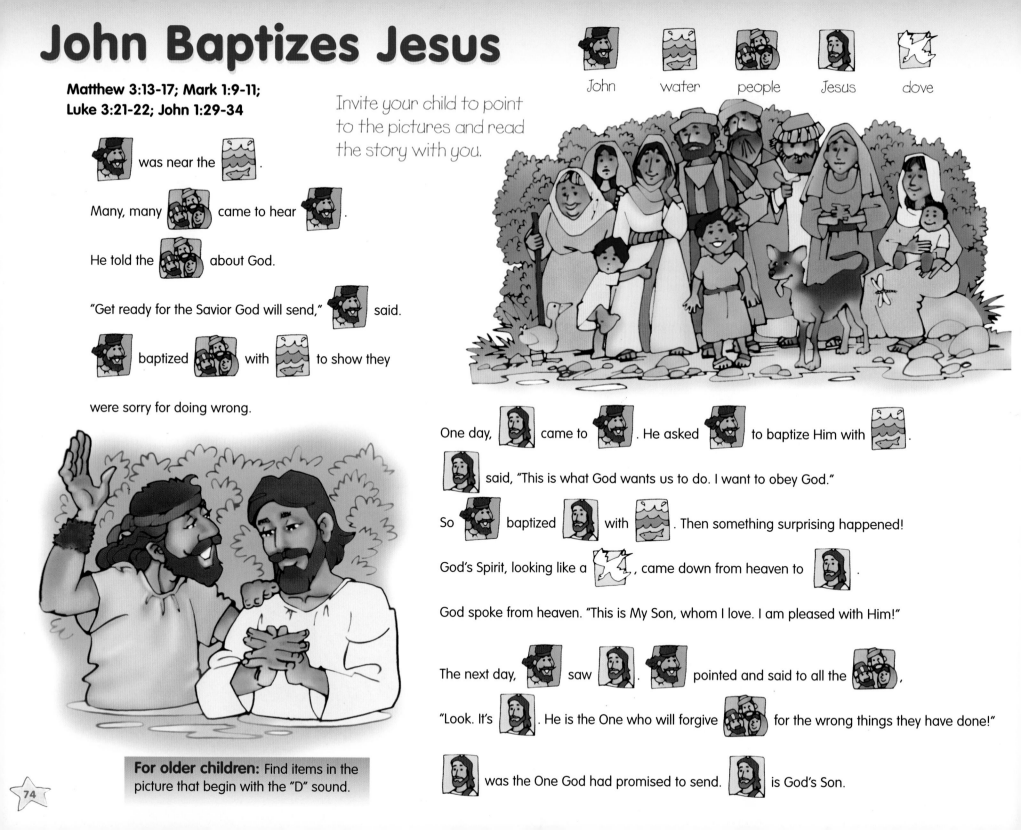

John   water   people   Jesus   dove

[John] was near the [water].

Many, many [people] came to hear [John].

He told the [people] about God.

"Get ready for the Savior God will send," [John] said.

[John] baptized [people] with [water] to show they

were sorry for doing wrong.

For older children: Find items in the picture that begin with the "D" sound.

One day, [Jesus] came to [John]. He asked [John] to baptize Him with [water].

[Jesus] said, "This is what God wants us to do. I want to obey God."

So [John] baptized [Jesus] with [water]. Then something surprising happened!

God's Spirit, looking like a [dove], came down from heaven to [Jesus].

God spoke from heaven. "This is My Son, whom I love. I am pleased with Him!"

The next day, [John] saw [Jesus]. [John] pointed and said to all the [people],

"Look. It's [Jesus]. He is the One who will forgive [people] for the wrong things they have done!"

[Jesus] was the One God had promised to send. [Jesus] is God's Son.

Jesus Chooses Helpers

Matthew 4:18-22; Luke 5:27-28

Invite your child to join you in the described actions.

Jesus walked by the big blue Sea of Galilee. **Walk fingers**.

He saw some fishermen in their boats. **Shade eyes with hand**.

They were throwing their big fishing nets out into the water. **Pretend to throw nets**.

Jesus called, "Peter! Andrew!" **Cup hands around mouth**.

When Peter and Andrew saw Jesus, they pulled in their nets. **Pretend to pull in nets**.

They hurried to see Jesus. Jesus said, "Come and help Me tell people about God." Peter and Andrew went with Jesus. **Walk fingers**.

Peter and Andrew wanted to learn more about Jesus. They wanted to help others learn about Jesus, too. Now Jesus had two helpers. **Hold up two fingers**.

Later Jesus and His two friends saw two other fishermen. **Hold up two fingers**.

"James and John!" Jesus called. "Come with Me!" James and John were glad to go with Jesus. Now Jesus had four helpers. **Hold up four fingers**.

On another day, Jesus walked by a man named Matthew. Matthew was at work. "Follow Me, Matthew," said Jesus. Matthew got right up. **Pretend to get up**.

Now Jesus had FIVE friends to help Him! **Hold up five fingers**.

On other days, Jesus asked other people to be His helpers—until He had 1, 2, 3, 4, 5, 6, 7, 8, 9, 10, 11, 12 helpers. **Count on fingers**.

Jesus told His 12 helpers many things about God. Then He sent them to different towns so that they could tell other people about God. **Point away**.

Jesus' friends did just what Jesus said to do. They told other people about God!

For older children: What are some other words that begin with the same sound as the word "follow"? (Look for some in the story!)

Woman at the Well

John 4:3-42

Invite your child to clap and say the last line of each stanza along with you.
(Tip: These words can also be sung to the tune of "Here We Go 'Round the Mulberry Bush.")

Here is the well where the people come;
They get water so each has some.
But one woman comes to the well alone.
On this hot dusty day in Samaria.

Here is the stranger who rests at the well.
He asks for a drink, and He starts to tell
The woman about all the things she has done.
On this hot dusty day in Samaria.

Here is the woman. She's very surprised.
This man knows about her, but He is so kind!
The woman is wondering, *Who could He be*?
On this hot dusty day in Samaria.

It's Jesus who's talking! He's got a surprise.
The woman now listens, and her eyes grow wide.
Jesus says He's the Savior God promised to send.
On this hot dusty day in Samaria.

The woman is happy. She starts to run!
In the town she shouts, "Listen to me, everyone!
I found the Savior God promised to send."
On this hot dusty day in Samaria.

The people follow. *Are her words true*?
They come to the well. Then they're surprised, too,
For Jesus tells them more of God's love!
On this hot dusty day in Samaria.

They told the woman, "Now we believe.
The Savior God promised has come here indeed!
We're glad to know Jesus and hear of God's love."
On this hot dusty day in Samaria.

For older children: Look at the picture. Count how many people or animals might like a drink of water. How many other ways of using water can you think of?

A Sick Boy Is Made Well

John 4:46-53

My body hurt. My head was HOT!
Was my dad happy? He was NOT!
I could not even leave my bed.
I could not even lift my head!

I knew my son was very sick.
I knew I had to get help—quick!
I knew that Jesus was nearby.
So I RAN to the town. I had to TRY!

We saw the dad. We heard him say,
"Jesus! Heal my boy today!"
Would Jesus go? What would He do?
We were surprised. The dad was, too!

I told the father, "You may go.
This is what you need to know:
Your son will live. He will be fine."
That dad looked up. His eyes met Mine.
He believed My words were true.
He turned around and went home, too!

As you read each part of the story, invite your child to point to the person speaking.

Just then the boy sat up in bed.
He said, "I'm fine!" and shook his head.
We ran to find his dad to say,
"Your son has been made well today!"

Jesus' words had made me well.
What a story I can tell!

For older children: Point to and say each pair of rhyming words on the page.

Jesus' Prayer

Matthew 6:5-13; Mark 1:35-37; Luke 11:1-4

Invite your child to answer each question
before reading the next paragraph.

The sun crept up in the sky, brighter and brighter. It was time to get up! Jesus' friends rubbed their eyes. They yawned and stretched. They looked around. They didn't see Jesus. **Where could He be?**

Jesus' friends went out to look for Him. They called and they walked. They walked and they called. Finally, they came to a quiet place, away from people. That's where Jesus was! **But what was He doing?**

Jesus was praying! His friends were glad to find Him! They wanted Jesus to come with them. But they wanted something else, too. **What did they want?**

Jesus' friends didn't know how to pray the way Jesus prayed. Jesus' friends asked Him to teach them how to pray! **What did Jesus tell His friends?**

Jesus told His friends, "When you pray, pray like this: 'Our Father who is in heaven, we love and respect Your name. We want You to be King over us. Give us what we need today. Forgive the wrong things we do. We forgive everyone who has done wrong to us. Please protect us. Help us to do right. You are the King. You can do anything. Amen.'" **What name did Jesus tell His friends to call God?**

Jesus told His friends to call God their Father. He told His friends to ask God, our Father in Heaven, for whatever they need. **When can we talk to God?** Anytime!

For older children: How many times can you find the word "pray" hidden in the picture?

ells of God's Love

Whenever you say the words **worried** or **worry**, say "Uh-oh!" Invite your child to join you.

Matthew 6:25-34; Luke 12:22-31

Jesus sat on a hillside. He was talking to His friends.

Jesus knew that His friends **worried**.

Sometimes they **worried** about not having enough food to eat.

Sometimes they **worried** about not having enough clothes to wear.

Jesus pointed up. His friends looked up into the sky.

Some birds were flying there.

Jesus said to His friends, "Look at those birds.

They don't **worry**. They don't plant seeds in the fields.

They don't tend gardens to grow food.

Yet God feeds them. He makes sure they have food.

God feeds birds. He will feed you, too!"

Jesus' friends watched the birds. They thought about them.

Then Jesus picked up some flowers. They were bright colors!

"See these flowers?" He asked. "Think about them.

They don't **worry** about having clothes to wear.

But what the flowers wear is even more beautiful than a king's fanciest robe.

God gives them these beautiful clothes, even though they are only flowers.

God will give you clothes, too!"

Jesus smiled at His friends. He said, "God knows what you need.

Don't **worry**. God will take care of you!"

For older children: Find the circles and triangles in the picture.

79

Friends Help a Lame Man

Invite your child to join you in making the motions and singing the song.

Mark 2:1-12

We are four friends—one, two, three, four. **Hold up four fingers.**

Here's a friend, too. We have one more! **Count on fingers to five.**

Our friend couldn't walk. Our friend couldn't stand. **Shake head no.**

So we took him to Jesus. Each one gave a hand. **Pretend to lift and carry.**

The day grew hot. The road seemed long. **Wipe brow.**

But we did not stop. We sang this song:

> **(Sing to the tune of the "ABC Song.")**
>
> Jesus makes sick people well. He cares for us—we can tell.
>
> He loves us. We'll find a way to get our friend to Him today.

We found the place where Jesus taught. **Shade eyes to look.**

But get our friend near? We could not! **Shake head no.**

Up to the roof, what could we do? **Shrug shoulders.**

We dug a hole and lowered him through! We sang:

> **(Sing to the tune of the "ABC Song.")**
>
> Jesus makes sick people well. He cares for us—we can tell.
>
> He loves us. We'll find a way to get our friend to Him today.

Jesus watched our friend come down. **Look up.**

He smiled at us. He didn't frown! **Smile.**

He told our friend, "Get up and walk."

Our friend got up and walked right off! **Nod.**

Now all FIVE could walk away!

Hold up five fingers.

We laughed and skipped back home that day!

We sang:

> **(Sing to the tune of the "ABC Song.")**
>
> Jesus makes sick people well.
>
> He cares for us—we can tell.
>
> We brought you to Him—hooray!
>
> He made you well. You walked away!

For older children: Show a family member what you can do with your legs and feet!

Jesus Stops the Storm

Matthew 8:23-27; Mark 4:1,35-41

Ask your child to point to each item in the picture as you read about it.

This is the sea so calm and clear
That floated the little fishing boat
That Jesus and His friends sailed.

This is the place where Jesus slept
On a pillow the sailors kept
    On the sea so calm and clear
    That floated the little fishing boat
    That Jesus and His friends sailed.

These are the waves that splashed so high,
Filling the boat so nothing was dry
And making the fearful friends cry
    On the sea not so calm
    That tossed the little fishing boat
    That Jesus and His friends sailed.

These are the friends who hung on tight
And shouted at Jesus with all their might,
"Jesus, help! We're going to die!
Because the waves have splashed so high,
Filling the boat so nothing is dry!"
    On the sea not so calm
    That tossed the little fishing boat
    That Jesus and His friends sailed.

These are the words that Jesus said
To wind and waves roaring 'round His head:
"Peace! Be still!"

These are the waves gently rocking the boat.
It didn't sink; it was still afloat.
And Jesus stood smiling at His friends.
Jesus' great power had made the storm end
    On the sea so calm and clear
    That floated the little fishing boat
    That Jesus and His friends sailed!

For older children: How many fish can you count in the waves?

Jesus Feeds 5,000

Mark 6:30-44; John 6:1-14

Point to the pictures and let your child help you read the story.

Jesus   boy   basket   bread   fish   friends   crowd

The  was excited! He was going to go see ! His mother put and in his . The walked and walked to a place where a big sat listening to . The found a place to sit. He listened to , too. Late in the day, said to His , "We should feed these people." Philip said, "We can't feed such a big ! We don't have that much MONEY!" Andrew, one of Jesus' friends, said, " , a little here has a of two and five loaves of ." His mother had put a good lunch in the boy's .

"But," Andrew said to , "such a small lunch won't ever feed such a big !"

told His to have everyone sit down. He was going to do something WONDERFUL!

The little gave his lunch to . thanked God for the food.

Then He gave the food to His . They passed it to the hungry .

The ate and until he was full.

EVERYONE else in that big ate until they were full, too! They all had enough to eat.

There was even food left over! loved the people in the . He loved His .

He loved the . He gave them what they needed when they were hungry!

For older children: Which of the small pictures begin with the "B" sound? With the "F" sound? The "J" sound?

82

Jesus Heals a Blind Man

Invite your child to close his or her eyes whenever you say the word **blind** and to keep them closed until he or she hears the word **see**.

John 9:1-11,35-38

Let me tell you what happened to me!
Once, I was **blind**.
I couldn't work. I couldn't play.
All I did was sit and ask people to give me money.
I couldn't **see** anything at all.

There I sat, waiting and sad.
Then Jesus did a great thing!
He was walking past me. Then He stopped.
He told His friends God was going to do
    something wonderful!

Then Jesus made some cool mud.
He put the mud on my **blind** eyes.
He told me to walk to a pool of water and wash the mud away.
I walked and walked, feeling my way.

When I got to the pool, I washed off the mud.
And you know what happened?
I could **SEE**!
I could **see** the splashing water!
I could **see** my hands in front of my face!
I could **see** blue sky above me!
I began to dance and shout, "I can **SEE**! I can **SEE**!"

I ran back to where Jesus had been.
The people who knew me were all VERY surprised.
"You look like the **blind** man who used to sit right here!" they told me.
"I AM that man!" I laughed. "I WAS **blind**.
But now I can **SEE**! Jesus has done a great thing for me!"

For older children: Find all the things in the picture that begin with the "M" sound.

83

The Greatest of All

As you read the words, ask your child to point to either Jesus or the child in each picture.

Mark 9:33-37; Luke 9: 46-48

For older children: Count the number of people in each picture.

The Forgiving King

Matthew 18:21-35

Invite your child to point to the person speaking as you read this story Jesus told.

1
I worked for the **king**.
I owed the **king** a LOT of **money**.
One day the **king** told me,
"PAY me the **money** you owe NOW."
I was scared. I did NOT have the **money**!

2
My **servant** got on his knees.
He said, "O **king**, please wait!
I will pay you what I owe you. I promise!"
My **servant** did NOT have the **money**, I knew.
I wanted to be kind to him.
I said, "I **forgive** you.
You don't have to pay ANY **money**!"

3
WOW!
I was SO HAPPY!
The **king** FORGAVE me.
I didn't owe ANY **money** now!
But on my way home,
I FORGOT how happy I was!

5
When I heard what my **servant** had done,
I ordered him to come to me.
I said, "I **forgave** you.
You owed me a LOT of **money**.
But you did not **forgive** your friend a LITTLE **money**.
You were unkind. You will be punished!"
I had my unkind **servant** put in jail.

4
The **king's servant** saw me.
I owed him a LITTLE **money**.
He grabbed me and said,
"WHERE is the **money** you owe me? Pay NOW!"
I was scared! I said, "Please wait!
I will pay you what I owe you. I promise!"
The **king's servant** wasn't kind.
He got ANGRY. He had me put in JAIL!

God forgives us. He wants us to love and forgive other people,
even when they are unkind. We can show God's love
by treating others kindly.

For older children: Count the number of times you see the words "king," "servant," "money" and "forgive."

85

The Good Samaritan

Luke 10:25-37

Jesus told this story to teach us to show love to anyone who needs help.

A man was going on a trip. **Walk your fingers.**

As he walked, some men jumped on him. **Jump fingers.**

They beat him up and took his money. **Make grabbing motion.**

The man lay on the ground. He couldn't even get up! **Lay head to the side.**

The man's head hurt. **Rub head.**

But he heard something! **Cup hand behind ear.**

Someone was walking near him! **Walk fingers.**

The hurt man waited. Would this person help him? **Hold hands up questioningly.**

But the traveler hurried on his way! **Walk fingers quickly.**

He DIDN'T do anything to help! **Shake head no.**

The hurt man groaned. He hurt all over! **Look sad.**

He heard MORE footsteps. **Cup hand behind ear.**

Would THIS person help? The footsteps stopped. **Walk fingers and then stop.**

THIS traveler LOOKED at the hurt man. **Twist fingers to "look."**

BUT this traveler DIDN'T do anything to help. **Shake head no.**

He hurried on HIS way, too! **Walk fingers quickly.**

The hurt man must have been VERY sad. **Look sad.**

He could only lie on the ground. **Lay head to the side.**

But then he heard a clippety-clop sound. **Cup hand behind ear.**

A donkey was coming. **Make donkey ears with your fingers.**

Would the person on the donkey help him? **Hold hands up questioningly.**

The donkey stopped. A man got off the donkey. **Walk fingers.**

He gave the hurt man a drink. **Offer drink.**

He put medicine on the hurt man's sores. **Pat hand.**

He wrapped bandages around the hurts. **Pretend to wrap your hand.**

Then the man lifted the hurt man onto the donkey. **Pretend to lift something.**

He took the hurt man to a safe place to stay. **Walk fingers.**

He paid for the hurt man to be taken care of. **Pay money.**

The man on the donkey SHOWED God's love. **Nod.**

He was kind to the hurt man who needed help! **Hug.**

Invite your child to make the motions with you as you read this story Jesus told.

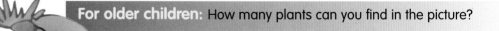

For older children: How many plants can you find in the picture?

The Good Shepherd

Luke 15:3-7

Invite your child to guess the words in red as you read this story Jesus told.

A good shepherd always loves his **sheep**.
He watches when they play.
At night he guards them while they **sleep**.
He never runs away.

He finds good grass for his sheep to **eat**.
He knows just what they need.
He finds cool water that is clean and **sweet**.
The sheep follow where he leads.

Every night he counts his **sheep**.
He knows each one by name.
If one is lost, he cannot **sleep**!
He loves each sheep the same.

He climbs up mountains, looking all **around**,
And calls the sheep by its name.
When the sheep is finally **found**,
It's glad the shepherd came.

He gently lifts the frightened **sheep**
Up, up into his arms.
The sheep is safe; it falls **asleep**!
There, it's safe from harm.

The shepherd brings it to the **fold**.
The sheep runs right inside.
It knows it's safe and won't be **cold**;
The shepherd sleeps beside.

Jesus told us that God loves us.
He is loving and kind like the good shepherd!
We can show God's love to others.

For older children: How many sheep can you count?

The Loving Father

As you read the story, ask your child to point to the pictures that show the story action.

Luke 15:11-24

The son wanted his money,
But he didn't want his dad.
His dad gave him the money,
Although his dad was sad.
Now the son had money—
More than he'd ever had!

The son went far from home;
He had a lot of fun.
He liked to spend his money—
Made friends with everyone.
One day he was surprised.
His money was all gone!

The son was awfully hungry!
He started tending pigs.
Working in that pigpen,
His sadness became big!
"I'm sorry I left home," he said.
"Will my dad still take me back?"

Even if his dad
Didn't want him for a son,
He'd ask to be Dad's hired man,
So he headed for his home.
But before he even got there,
His dad began to run!

He hugged his son and kissed him,
Gave him a ring and clothes.
Dad also planned a party,
Which only goes to show
That God is like that daddy.
We're always welcomed home!

For older children: Count the spotted pigs and then the plain pigs. How many muddy pigs are there? Clean pigs?

One Man Thanks Jesus

Invite your child to help you read the story using the rebus pictures.

 Jesus   10 sick men   road   one man families homes

Luke 17:11-19

 sat beside the 🛣️ . These 👥 were sad. Their sickness meant they could not go to their 🏠 . They could not be with their 👨‍👩‍👧 .

One day, 👤 came down the 🛣️ . The 👥 said to each other, "Look! It's 👤 !" The 👥 must have heard that 👤 could make sick people well.

So the 👥 began to shout, " 👤 ! MASTER! Please help us!"

👤 stopped. He looked at the 👥 . He said to the 👥 , "Go and show people you are well now."

The 👥 got VERY excited. They began to run. Now they could go to their 🏠 . They could be with their 👨‍👩‍👧 ! And as they ran, they could see that they were WELL! They were NOT 👥 anymore!

Nine men ran and ran. But 👤 stopped. He turned around. He looked at 👤 . The 👤 began to run—right back to where 👤 was!

This 👤 who had been sick knelt down in front of 👤 .

He thanked 👤 for making him well!

For older children: What items do you have 10 or more of in your house?

89

Jesus Loves Children

Invite your child to join you in saying and motioning **stop** and **go**.

Matthew 19:13-15; Mark 10:13-16

It's a happy day for some families! They will **go** to do something very important They will **go** to see Jesus!

Mothers and fathers say, "Time to **stop** playing. Get ready to **go**!" Parents help their children wash their faces and brush their hair. Soon, everyone is ready to **go**.

"Let's **go**," say the mothers. "We won't **stop** very often on the way. We want to see Jesus SOON!"

The families walk together. They want to **go** see Jesus NOW! Parents carry tired ones so that they don't have to **stop**.

Soon, they see some people. They ask, "Is that where Jesus is? Let's **go**!"

The children hurry. The parents hurry. They do not **stop**. They want to get to Jesus!

But as the families **go** close to where Jesus is, Jesus' friends step in their way. The men say, "**STOP**! Don't bother Jesus. He is too busy to see children. **Go** away!"

The children and parents turn around. Slowly, they **go** away. They are very sad.

Jesus sees them **go**. And Jesus says to His friends who told them to **stop**, "Let the children come to Me! Never tell them to **go** away!"

Then Jesus motions for the children to come close. He takes them by the hand. He holds them in His lap. He prays for them. He doesn't want them to **stop** coming to Him. He doesn't want them to **go** away! Jesus loves children!

For older children: Read the story again, adding your own actions for some other words.

A Rich Man's Question

Matthew 19:16-26; Mark 10:17-27;
Luke 18:18-27

As you read the story, invite your child to imitate the face beside each paragraph.

I am a rich young man. I heard JESUS was coming to town.
When I saw Jesus, I was EXCITED! I knelt down in front of Him.
I asked, "Teacher, what should I do so that
   I can live forever?"

Jesus smiled. He looked into my face.
He said, "Do what God says to do. Do not kill anyone.
Do not take anything that isn't yours. Do not tell lies.
Love and obey your father and mother.
Love other people the same way
   you love yourself."
I smiled. I said, "I have done all of
   these things since I was just a little boy!"

But then Jesus SURPRISED me.
He said, "There is still one thing you need to do.
Sell what you have.
Give the money to poor people.
Then come and follow Me."

WOW! My face began to look VERY sad.
I didn't want to sell ANYTHING.
I wanted to KEEP it ALL!

I walked away slowly. I could still hear Jesus.
He said to His friends, "It is very hard for
   people who love money to love God."

Jesus' friends were surprised! They asked,
"Then who CAN have life that lasts forever?"
"NO ONE can do it alone," Jesus said.
"You must have God's help to live forever."

I walked and thought about what I heard Jesus say.
Only God can help us do good things.
Only God can help us live forever.
Only God can help us share with others.

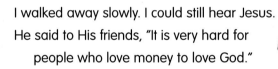

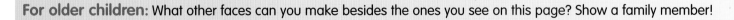
For older children: What other faces can you make besides the ones you see on this page? Show a family member!

Jesus Loves Zacchaeus

Luke 19:1-10

Invite your child to do the
motions with you. Repeat
the poem several times.

Zacchaeus heard the people say,

"Jesus is coming here today."

Zacchaeus thought, *What will I do?*

I sure want to see Jesus, too.

He thought of just the way to see—

Zacchaeus climbed up in a tree!

When Jesus saw him in the tree,

He said, "Please come down here to Me.

I want to be your friend today."

And Zacchaeus hurried to obey.

For older children: Count the leaves
that have spots on them.

Jesus Enters Jerusalem

Matthew 21:1-11,15-16;
Mark 11:1-10

Do the motions below when you see the words in color. Invite your child to imitate you.

Look   **Listen**

Look! See the crowds? They are all walking.
Listen to the people. What are they shouting?
"Jesus is coming! He's coming this way!"

Look! Here comes Jesus! He is riding a donkey.
Listen. I hear singing! The people around Jesus are singing an old, old song:
"Hosanna! God bless the One who comes in the name of the Lord!"

Look! The people in Jerusalem hear the singing, too.
They are running to join the others! It looks like a parade!

Look! Some people cut branches from the trees.
They laid them on the road. Others laid their coats on the road.
The road looks like a beautiful carpet for Jesus to ride over!

Look! There goes Jesus. Let's sing to Him, too!
Listen! "Hosanna! God bless the One who comes in the name of the Lord!"

Look! Jesus is walking into the Temple. Men with ANGRY faces are there! They don't want us to praise Jesus.
Listen! They growl at Jesus, "Do you hear what these children are singing?" "Yes," Jesus laughs. "Haven't you read what it says in God's Word? God said the children would praise Me!"

Look! Jesus is here.
Listen! Let's sing to Jesus again! He is glad to hear children praise Him!

For older children: How many people in these pictures are waving branches? How many are shouting or singing?

People Praise Jesus

Matthew 21:1-11,15-16; Luke 19:28-38

Walk your fingers whenever you say the word **walk**. Cup your hands around your mouth whenever you say the word **shout**. Invite your child to copy your motions.

Jesus told his friends, "**Walk** to the place I tell you. You will find a donkey there. Untie it and bring it to Me."

Jesus' friends **walked**.
They found the donkey just as Jesus had told them.
They brought the donkey back to Jesus.
Jesus' friends spread their coats on the donkey's back.
Jesus sat on the donkey.
The donkey began to **walk** down the road to Jerusalem.
Jesus' friends came, too.

Many other people **walked** on the road.
They began to **shout**, "Look! Jesus is coming!"

People wanted Jesus to know they were glad to see Him!
They **shouted** praises to Jesus.
They **walked** to trees and cut down branches.
Some people laid these branches in the road.
Some people took off their coats.
They laid their coats on the road so that
      the road looked like a colorful carpet!

People **shouted** praises to Jesus.
They **walked** with Him and waved branches.
It looked like a big parade!

Jesus **walked** into the Temple.
Many children **walked** with Him.
They **shouted** praises to Jesus.
It was a wonderful day in the big city of Jerusalem!
People everywhere showed love for Jesus
      by praising Him.
It's good to praise and show love for Jesus!

For older children: How many branches can you find in this picture?

The Poor Woman's Gift

Mark 12:41-44

I am a widow. That means my husband is dead. This is all the money I have. I am glad to give this money. I want to show God I love Him.

I have lots of money. I like to hear the loud jingling noise it makes when I put it into the offering box! I still have plenty of money at home.

Did you see the widow? Did you see her two coins? She gave more than the rich man did.

But she only put two coins into the box.

The rich man still had lots of money left at home. Those two little coins were all the money the widow had.

For older children: How many coins can you count in this picture?

Jesus Dies and Lives Again

Make faces as indicated.
Invite your child to join you.

**Matthew 26:1-4,47-50; 27:11-66;
John 18—20:20**

One day Jesus told His friends,
"Some people are going to take Me away.
I am going to be killed." **Make a sad face**.

Jesus knew that this would be sad and scary.
But He knew it was part of God's good plan.
He knew He wouldn't STAY dead. **Smile**.

The people who wanted to kill Jesus
    came to the place where Jesus prayed.
Jesus let them take Him away.
He let them hurt Him and kill Him on a cross.
Make a sad face.

Jesus' friends took Jesus' body and
    put it into a tomb, like a little cave.
Some men rolled a very BIG stone over
    the doorway.
Make a crying face.

Three days later, a lady named Mary
    came to the tomb.
The BIG stone had been moved!
Make a surprised face.

She looked inside the tomb.
There were two ANGELS in the tomb!
One angel asked, "Why are you sad?"

Mary said, "Jesus is gone.
I don't know where He is!"

Then Mary turned around. Oops!
She almost bumped into someone.

"Mary!" the person said.
Mary knew that voice.

Who WAS it? It was JESUS!
Jesus was ALIVE!
He was standing right there in front
    of her!
Jesus told Mary, "Go and tell the others."
Make a glad face.

Mary was GLAD!
She RAN to tell Jesus' other friends!

"Jesus is ALIVE!" she said.
"I have SEEN Him!"

Some of Jesus' friends didn't believe
    Mary. **Make a sad face**.

But soon, they saw Jesus, too!
Then they were GLAD!
Make a glad face.

For older children: How many times can you find Jesus' name in the story?

The Empty Tomb

Matthew 28:1-10; Luke 22:2; 23:33—24:9; John 19:38-42

For older children: Show with your face and arms the actions of a person in these pictures. See if someone can guess who you are pretending to be.

97

The Road to Emmaus

Luke 24:13-35

Invite your child to join you in saying the repeating words.

We are traveling together on this **road, road, road.**
We feel sad, like we're carrying a very heavy load.
A man walks beside us on the **way, way, way.**
He asks, "May I walk along with you today?"

We begin talking as we **go, go, go.**
We tell the man news that we think He should know.
We tell of Jesus dying. We are **sad, sad, sad.**
Then this man starts talking. His words make us glad!

Now the sun is setting, going **down, down, down.**
We're going to eat and sleep in Emmaus town.
We ask the man beside us to **stay, stay, stay.**
He amazes us at dinner when we hear Him pray!

The man picks up a piece of **bread, bread, bread.**
He gives thanks to God as He bows His head.
He breaks the bread for us to **share, share, share.**
Now we can see that it's JESUS sitting there!

We're GLAD to see Him. Now we **know, know, know!**
Jesus is alive! But it's time for Him to go.
We don't see Him anymore, but we're still **glad, glad, glad!**
We run to tell the others, "He's ALIVE! Do not be sad!"

For older children: Have a family member read the story again while you act it out!

Thomas Sees Jesus

John 20:19-31

Invite your child to say the repeated words with you.

Jesus died. But three days later, Jesus lived again!

When His friends saw Jesus, they were **glad, glad, GLAD**!

But one friend of Jesus still was **sad, sad, SAD**.

Thomas was not there when Jesus came to visit.

Later, Thomas's friends saw him.

They said, "Listen. Listen. LISTEN!

"We've seen Jesus. He's not dead.

He is **risen, risen, RISEN!**"

But Thomas said, "I don't believe you. **No. No. NO**!

Unless I see and touch Him, I won't believe it's so!"

Then seven days later, Jesus came to them again.

This time, Thomas was there, too.

The doors were **locked, locked, LOCKED**.

But that did not stop Jesus.

Right into the room He **walked, walked, WALKED**!

Thomas stared. It was Jesus; he could **see, see, SEE**!

Jesus said to Thomas, "Touch Me and believe!"

Thomas bowed at Jesus' feet. "My Lord and God!" he said.

Now Thomas KNEW his friends were right. Jesus was NOT dead!

And still the same good news is true: JESUS IS **alive, alive, ALIVE**!

For older children: Find the items in the picture that begin with the sound of the letter "B."

Jesus Lives Today

Matthew 28:16-20; John 21:1-14; Acts 1:3-11

Invite your child to read with you by saying the pictured word.

Jesus · cross · friends · mountain · sky · heaven · angels · cloud

Jesus died on a [cross]. His [friends] were very sad. But [Jesus] didn't stay dead.

After **3** days, [Jesus] came alive again! That made His [friends] GLAD!

[Jesus] walked and talked with His [friends] for **40** more days. [Jesus] told His

[friends] He was going back to [heaven] soon. He promised His [friends]

He would always love them. He told them to wait in Jerusalem until He sent the

Holy Spirit to help them. **1** day it was time for [Jesus] to go back to [heaven].

[Jesus] and His [friends] walked together to a [mountain]. Up on the [mountain],

[Jesus] said to His [friends], "Remember that I am always with you. I will take care

of you. And after I have gone back to [heaven], tell people everywhere I love them."

Then [Jesus] began to rise up into the [sky]! His [friends] were surprised!

[Jesus] went up and up until He was in a [cloud]. His [friends] couldn't see [Jesus]

anymore. Suddenly, **2** [angels] were standing beside Jesus' [friends]. The [angels]

said, "Why are you standing here looking into the [sky]? [Jesus] will come back

someday, just as you saw Him go!" Jesus' [friends] were happy! [Jesus] was going to

come back someday! Until that day they knew [Jesus] would take care of them and help them.

For older children: Count to 40. What other numbers do you see in this story?

101

The Lame Man Walks

Acts 3:1-16

Once my legs could not **walk** or **run**.
I could not work or help my friends.
I could only **lie** on a mat.
So I lay by the Temple gate.

Every day people **walked** past me.
Every day I asked them for money
   so that I could buy food and clothes.
One day, two men **walked** up to me.
I asked for money, like I always did.
One man said, "Look at us."
I looked up. *Would he give
   me money?*

Use your fingers to imitate legs doing story actions in colored type. Invite your child to do actions with you.

The man who **walked** up to me was Peter.
He looked into my eyes.
He said, "I have no money to give you.
But I'll give you what I DO have.
In Jesus' name, **walk**!"
Peter pulled me to my feet.
My legs were strong! I **STOOD**!
I could **tiptoe**. I could **march**.
I could **skip**. I could **jump**!
I **walked** into the Temple all by myself!
I surprised everyone!
Peter and John obeyed God.
They helped me.
And God made my legs **walk**!

For older children: Show how you can do these story actions: walk, run, tiptoe, march, skip and jump.

Barnabas Shares

Invite your child to say the repeating line with you.

Acts 4:32-37

We're people who love Jesus. We're all part of God's family. **We share everything!**

We love each other. We help each other. **We share everything!**

I did not have a coat.

I had two coats. I gave one to him. **We share everything!**

I was hungry.

We had food. We invited her to dinner! **We share everything!**

We need a place to stay.

Welcome! We asked them to stay with us! **We share everything!**

Sometimes, we sell land we own.

We give the money to God's family so that NO ONE needs money. **We share everything!**

Thank you, Barnabas!

God's family is growing. It is good to see that **We share everything!**— "Some for you and some for me!"

For older children: Say the beginning sound of each item that was shared.

103

Food for Widows

Clap your hands whenever you read the word **more**. Invite your child to join you.

Acts 6:1-7

Every day **more** and **more** people were hearing about Jesus.

More and **more** people were becoming part of God's family.

And **more** and **more** people were sharing with each other.

God's people were showing each other **more** and **more** love!

But there was a problem. Some women were hungry!

They needed **more** food.

Jesus' friends wanted God's family to have **more** love,
  not **more** hunger!

So they asked everyone to choose some special helpers.

These helpers would be sure everyone got enough food.

They chose one, two, three, four. But they needed even **more**!

They chose three **more** helpers. Now there were five, six, seven helpers.

Seven helpers were enough. They didn't need **more**.

God's family was glad to have helpers so that
  they could share **more** and **more**!

104

For older children: Find and circle the animals in the picture.

Philip and the Ethiopian

Acts 8:26-40

Philip was a helper who made sure everyone in God's family had enough food.

One day an angel came to talk to Philip.

An angel is God's special messenger.

The angel said, "Go and walk on the road that leads away from the city."

Put your finger on the road.

Invite your child to find items in the picture as you read the story.

Philip obeyed God right away!

He went out and walked on that road!

Philip heard the sound of horses' hooves.

He saw horses pulling a chariot, a cart to ride in.

Put your finger on the horses.

There was a man inside the chariot.

He was an important man from a faraway country.

The man was reading a scroll.

The scroll was God's Word.

Put your finger on the scroll.

God told Philip to run up to the chariot.

Philip asked the man inside,

"Do you understand the words you're reading?"

"No! I need help to understand these
      words!" the man said.

Put your finger on the man.

Philip climbed into the chariot.

He read the words on the scroll.

The words told about Jesus.

Philip told the man all the good news about Jesus!

Put your finger on Philip.

The man was happy to hear the good news that Jesus loved him!

He believed Jesus is God's Son.

He was glad Philip had obeyed God and told him the good news.

Philip was glad, too!

For older children: How many circles can you find?

105

Paul Meets Jesus

Acts 9:1-20*

Ask your child to find each face as you read the story.
Make the facial expression with your child.

God's family was growing!

Many people were learning about and loving Jesus.

These people were happy. **Find the happy face.**

But one man named Paul did not love Jesus.

Paul was very mean to Jesus' friends.

Paul was angry. **Find the angry face.**

Paul wanted to stop the people who loved Jesus.

So Paul decided to travel to a big city.

There he would catch Jesus' friends and put them in jail!

Jesus' friends were sad. **Find the sad face.**

Paul and his friends traveled.

But when they came near to that big city, a bright
   light shone!

Paul fell to the ground. He couldn't see!

Then Paul heard a voice! It was Jesus!

"Why are you hurting Me?" Jesus said.

Hurting Jesus' friends hurt Jesus, too!

Paul was surprised! **Find the surprised face.**

Paul asked Jesus what to do.

Jesus told him to go into the city and to wait there.

While Paul waited, Jesus told His friend Ananias to go to Paul.

Ananias was worried and afraid. **Find the fearful face.**

"Paul came here to HURT us!" Ananias said.

Jesus told Ananias it would be all right. So Ananias obeyed!

He prayed for Paul. Then Paul could see again!

Now Paul loved Jesus and was very happy. **Find the happy face.**

Paul told people everywhere that Jesus is God's Son!

***Note to parents:** To lessen the confusion for children, the name Paul instead of Saul is used here.

For older children: Count the squares and triangles in the picture.

Paul Escapes in a Basket

Acts 9:20-28

Squeeze your child's hand each time you read the word friend.

Once Paul had wanted to hurt Jesus' **friends**.

But Paul learned that Jesus is God's Son.

Now Paul was Jesus' **friend**, too!

Paul went all over town, telling people that
Jesus is God's Son.

But some people were NOT Jesus' **friends**.

Paul's words made them angry.

They said, "We must STOP Paul. We will catch him and kill him!"

They made a plan. The city had a high wall all around it.

The only way to go out was through the gates.

They would wait at the gates for Paul and CATCH him.

But Paul's **friends** found out about the plan.

They said, "We can't let anyone hurt our friend Paul!"

Paul's **friends** thought of a plan to help Paul.

They took a great big basket and a long, long rope.

Paul's **friends** took him to an opening in the city wall.

Paul got into the big basket.

His **friends** tied the long rope around it.

They began to let the basket down the outside of the wall.

It was scary! But Paul knew God loved him.

When the basket touched the ground, Paul got out.

He waved to his **friends**. They had helped keep him safe!

For older children: Name your friends. What letter does
each friend's name begin with?

Peter Helps Dorcas

Acts 9:32-43

Invite your child to name each rebus picture as you read.

 Dorcas  men Dorcas's friends clothes   Peter

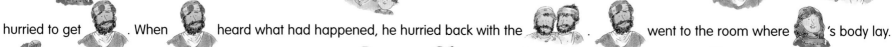

 was a very kind lady.  loved to sew. She made 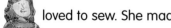 for other people. Dorcas's friends were glad when  gave them coats to keep them warm.

One day  got very sick. She got so sick that she died. Dorcas's friends were sad. One friend must have said, "We need to get Peter!" So two men hurried to get Peter. When Peter heard what had happened, he hurried back with the men. Peter went to the room where 's body lay.

Dorcas's friends were VERY sad. They were crying. They showed Peter the clothes kind  had made for them. Then Peter asked Dorcas's friends to leave the room.

Peter prayed to God. After he prayed, he said, ", get up!"  opened her eyes. She sat up. And she GOT UP! Dorcas's friends came into the room.

There was —and she was ALIVE! Everyone knew  had been dead. Dorcas's friends were all so HAPPY! God had made their friend ALIVE again!

For older children:
Count the pictures of Dorcas.

Peter Escapes from Prison

Acts 12:1-18

Do the motions indicated as you read the story. Invite your child to imitate your actions.

Peter was put into prison.
His friends knew this wasn't right.
But what could they do to help him?
They could pray all day and all
    night!

They asked God to rescue Peter,
To show His love and His care.
So God sent an angel to
    Peter
To answer all of their prayers.

Peter was chained between two guards;
Then the chains fell off of his feet!
Quickly, quietly, he got up
And the guards both stayed
    asleep.

Peter rose and put on his
    sandals;
He put on his belt and his coat.
The angel led him through the
    prison.
No one in the place even woke!

The heavy gate swung
    wide open.
Peter stepped out, and he was free!
He knew God always was with him.
In jail or wherever he would be.

Peter ran then to tell all his friends
The great thing God had just done!
He knocked and knocked
    on the door
And waited for someone to come.

Rhoda ran to answer the knocking.
She asked, "Who's at the door?"
Peter answered, "It's me! I'm Peter!
Let me in; I'll tell you some more!"

Rhoda ran to tell those who were praying,
"Peter's here!" She was so
    surprised!
She forgot to let poor Peter
    come in.
He kept knocking and waiting outside!

At last the door was opened.
Peter smiled and said,
    "Yes, it's true!
God brought me out
    of that prison.
Tell everyone what our
    God can do."

For older children: Listen to the story again and try to make the motions without looking at the pictures.
What other motions can you think of?

Paul Helps a Lame Man

Acts 14:8-20

Invite your child to join you as you say the word "walking" whenever you see a **foot**, "listening" whenever you see an **ear**, and "looking" whenever you see **eyes**.

Paul and Barnabas were 👣 , 👣 , 👣 from town to town. Everywhere they went, they told 👂 people about Jesus and helped sick people.

Paul and Barnabas came 👣 , 👣 to a town called Lystra. They told the 👂 people there that Jesus is God's Son. They told how Jesus made sick people well. Paul was 👁 👁 at one man in the crowd who was 👂 . This man had never been 👣 in his whole life. His feet didn't work. The 👂 man was 👁 👁 back at Paul. Paul could see that the man who had never been 👣 believed God could make his feet well!

So Paul said to the man, "Stand up on your feet!" The 👂 man was surprised! Suddenly, his feet worked. He jumped up and began 👣 , 👣 , 👣 ! He probably hopped and danced! God had made his feet well!

The people in the crowd were 👁 👁 at the man 👣 , 👣 , 👣 ! The people got VERY excited! They thought Paul and Barnabas had healed the man! But Paul and Barnabas asked the people to be 👂 as they spoke.

"We are just people like everyone else," they said. "Only God could make the man's feet go 👣 , 👣 , 👣 ."

Soon, Paul and Barnabas were 👣 , 👣 , 👣 to the next town. They were on their way to tell more 👂 people about God's love. They were 👁 👁 for ways to help people know about Jesus, who can make lame feet go 👣 , 👣 , 👣 !

For older children: How many ears do you count? Eyes? Feet?

Paul Tells About Jesus

As you read the name of a color, invite your child to point to items of that color on the page.

Acts 16:9-15

I am Paul, a friend of Jesus. Let me tell you why I am here by this blue river.

One night I was sleeping. The sky was black with yellow stars. I had a dream.
In the dream, a man said, "Come to my country and help us!"

When I woke, the sky was pink with the dawn. I told my friends about the dream.
We decided to go to the man's country to tell the good news about Jesus.

We packed our things quickly! Then we walked down the gray dusty road to the sea.
We got on a big brown ship. Soon we were sailing on the sea.

Finally, we got to this country. There was a big city with high white walls nearby.
We found a place with green grass by the blue river. We met some women here.
They had come to the blue river to pray.

I began to tell these women the good news about Jesus! One lady named Lydia believed my words.
She became part of God's family! Lydia sold purple cloth. She invited us to stay at her home.
We told even MORE people about Jesus. He loves everyone!

For older children: Can you find in the room where you are each of the colors mentioned in the story?

111

Singing in Jail

Acts 16:16-34

As you read, sing the colored words to the tune of "Jingle Bells." Invite your child to join you.

For older children: Using a tune you know, make up your own song about Jesus and sing it to your family.

Paul and Silas were in a city, telling about Jesus. But some people got angry at them. The leaders of the city had Paul and Silas beaten and put in jail. Their feet were locked between big blocks of wood. They hurt all over!

But Paul and Silas knew God cared about them.
Paul and Silas started to sing songs to God!

> **We will tell our good news: God has done great things.**
> **Jesus loves us all today. That is why we sing!**

Late that night, Paul and Silas still sang and sang, louder and louder.
All the other prisoners could hear the songs about the good news of Jesus!

> **We will tell our good news: God has done great things.**
> **Jesus loves us all today. That is why we sing!**

All of a sudden, the ground began to shake! It shook harder and HARDER!
The doors to the jail cells popped open! The locks broke! The chains fell off!
All the prisoners were FREE!

The jailer asked, "What must I do to be saved?"
Paul and Silas said, "Believe in the Lord Jesus Christ. You will be saved!"
The jailer was GLAD! He took Paul and Silas to his own house.

Then the jailer's whole family believed in Jesus! They made a big meal and washed Paul and Silas's sores. Now they could sing with Paul and Silas!

> **We will tell our good news: God has done great things.**
> **Jesus loves us all today. That is why we sing!**

The next morning, Paul and Silas started walking to another city.
They were ready to tell other people about Jesus—by talking, praying and singing!

> **We will tell our good news: God has done great things.**
> **Jesus loves us all today. That is why we sing!**

Paul Obeys God

Acts 21:17—22

God had told Paul, "Go and tell people the good news about Jesus." **Point**.
So Paul obeyed! Paul and his friends traveled to many places. **Walk fingers**.
They told people, "Jesus is God's Son." **Cup hands around mouth**.
One day Paul and his friends came to Jerusalem. **Walk fingers**.

Paul told Jesus' friends in Jerusalem, "God has helped me tell people about Jesus.
Now MANY people love Jesus. They are part of God's family, too!" **Nod**.

Later, Paul went to the Temple to pray. Some people saw Paul there.
These people were ANGRY that Paul told about Jesus. **Point**.

They shouted, "Look! There is Paul! This man does not obey God's rules!"
Some men dragged Paul out of the Temple into a big angry crowd of people.
The people shouted so loud that some soldiers came. They thought Paul must have
   done something wrong! So they put chains around Paul's hands and feet. **Grab wrist**.

Then the soldiers asked the people, "Who is this man? What has he done?"
Everyone shouted even MORE! The soldiers couldn't understand any of the shouting.
So they took Paul away from the Temple. But the crowd followed! **Walk fingers**.

Then Paul asked, "May I talk to these people?" The leader said Paul could talk.
So Paul stood on the steps until the people became quiet. **Put finger to lips**.

Paul said, "I used to hurt people who loved Jesus. But now I love Jesus, too.
God has told me to tell all people the good news that Jesus is God's Son.
And I am obeying God." **Nod**.

Even though the people were angry, Paul obeyed God and told them about Jesus.

For older children: Say the title of this Bible story in as many ways (loudly, softly, whispering, singing, chanting, etc.) as you can!

A Boy Helps Paul

Acts 23:12-35

As you read each part of the story, invite your child to point to the person speaking.

I'm one of 40 men who promised not to eat or drink until Paul is DEAD.
We've planned to trick the soldiers, so Paul will leave jail.
Then we'll get him!

I'm Paul's nephew.
I heard about the awful plan those 40 men made!
They wanted to kill my uncle!
So I went right to Uncle Paul and told him.
He sent me to the commander.

I'm Paul. I had been telling people about Jesus!
But some angry people had me put into jail.

I'm the commander.
This boy, Paul's nephew, came to me.
He told me about the trick those 40 men planned.
They want to kill Paul.
But it's my job to keep him safe.
So I'll make SURE he's safe when he leaves the jail!

I'm a soldier who rides a horse.
Our commander is sending 70 of us with Paul tonight.
He's sending 200 soldiers and 200 men carrying spears, too!
We'll put Paul right in the middle of all of us.
Those 40 men waiting to hurt Paul will never see him!
It's a good thing Paul's nephew told us about the plan.
Paul will be safe!

For older children: How many numbers can you find in the words? How many names?

Safe in a Shipwreck

Acts 27

Point to the pictures and let your child help you read the story.

Paul   ship   water   wind   waves   clouds   rain

[Paul] and his friends climbed onto a big [ship]. They sailed far across the [water]. The [wind] blew the [ship] far away from land. Soon, [Paul] and the other people on the [ship] saw only [water].

Then one day, the [wind] blew harder and HARDER. The [waves] splashed higher and HIGHER. The [waves] lifted the [ship] way UP. Then the [waves] pushed the [ship] way DOWN! The [water] splashed high and WHOOSHED into the [ship]. The sky was full of dark [clouds] that poured [rain]. For days and days the people on the [ship] were afraid. They thought they were going to die!

But [Paul] called them together. He said, "Don't be afraid. No one will be hurt. God sent an angel to tell me God will keep us all safe. Cheer up!"

The [wind] kept blowing. Finally, the [ship] came close to land! [Paul] gave the people bread. He told them to eat, so they would be strong and ready. Then—CRASH!

The strong [waves] broke the [ship] apart. The people jumped into the [water]. They grabbed pieces of the broken [ship] and floated through the [waves] to a little island. They were safe!

The people on the [ship] were glad [Paul] had shown love for them. [Paul] had told them what God had said. [Paul] had given them food. And God had taken care of everyone, just as [Paul] had said He would!

For older children: Make up an action for each rebus picture. Then read the story again using your actions!